A Natural History of
Christmas
❧
A Miscellany

Dr. Michael Leach has been a professional wildlife author and photographer since 1977. He has studied animals on all 7 continents and has written 24 natural history books; his photographs have been published in magazines and books in over 80 countries. He's written for publications such as *BBC Wildlife, The Observer Magazine* and *Country Life* and has filmed wildlife documentaries for both ITV and BBC. Michael is a favourite on the professional lecture circuit and has been described as a "unique wildlife humorist". **www.michael-leach.co.uk**

Dr. Meriel Lland lectures at Manchester Metropolitan University, she is a writer, photographer and artist with a fascination for the stories we tell of the natural world and the secrets those stories reveal of their tellers. She has travelled with reindeer in Scandinavia, elephants in Africa and camels in Morocco. A turtle dove once shared her garden. Her work - written and visual – has featured in books, magazines and newspapers nationally and internationally including *BBC Wildlife, The Daily Telegraph* and *RSPB Birds*. **www.meriellland.co.uk**

Acknowledgements
Meriel would like to thank David, Tolly, Todd and Deborah for their sharp focus, challenging questions, patience and unconditional kindness. And to Cheryl, who on one long ago Christmas Eve helped me hear sleigh bells – thank you. To Margaret and Peter – my parents - for helping me believe that one day I'd see the Northern Lights. You are forever my inspiration.

Previous page:
Lapland in midwinter is dominated by snow-covered fir trees. The great northern forests form a unique habitat, known as the taiga.

A Natural History of
Christmas
❧
A Miscellany

Michael Leach
&
Meriel Lland

Quandary Press

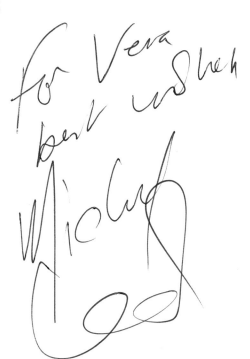

For Vera
best wishes

[signature]

ISBN 0-9540431-2-X

Published by Quandary Press

quandarypress@gmail.com

Designed and Typeset by Matthew Lloyd using 100% renewable electricity
matthew@thinkgraphic.co.uk

Set in Garamond

INTRODUCTION

Seasoned apple logs give off a sweet smell as they crackle and glow in the open fire. Above, on the old mantel, are cards from family and friends, showing robins perched on snowy boughs and teams of harnessed reindeer pulling a sleigh effortlessly across a starry sky. In the corner a young pine tree adds a sharp, green tang to the gentle scent of the apple wood, its evergreen branches decorated with stars and glass baubles that have been in the family for generations.

The table almost groans beneath the weight of a huge roast turkey, surrounded by the seasonal trimmings; cranberry sauce, bread sauce, sage and onion stuffing, roast potatoes, glazed carrots and Brussels sprouts. The wine is set to breathe on the dresser and, in the background, the ethereal voices of King's College choir can be heard singing "The 12 days of Christmas". In the kitchen a round, rich pudding simmers gently on the stove, while a bottle of brandy and sprig of holly lie ready on the table.

Eagerly awaited guests knock on a door dressed with a mossy wreath intertwined with long strands of ivy and gold ribbons, dotted with pine cones and holly berries. They step inside, out of the snow that is drifting steadily across the garden path, to stand – and be kissed – under a bunch of mistletoe tied with a red ribbon and hung from the ceiling. Each guest is handed a welcome glass of mulled wine and the sweet scent of sugar, oranges and cinnamon warms the air. Then the mince pies are offered around as everyone wishes their friends "Merry Christmas".

The modern Christmastide festival was shaped and styled by the Victorians.

This picture-perfect version of Christmas we recognise today is a Victorian invention. The celebrations as a whole would be alien to people from earlier times, although they might find many of the details oddly familiar. The Victorians gathered and knitted together myths, legends, foods and traditions from many periods in history and an unlikely number of apparently unconnected cultures. They produced a festival built of icons and beliefs imported from five continents. Discovering the footprints of these wanderings is the adventure of this book.

Christmas, meaning "Christ's Mass", is the yearly commemoration of the birth of Jesus Christ celebrated generally on December 25th. A feast central to the Christian calendar of rituals, it closes the Advent season (the time celebrating preparation for the immanent birth of Jesus) and initiates the twelve days of Christmastide, which ends after Twelfth Night (at which point the Magi visit the baby and reveal his divine nature). Christmas is a civil holiday in many of the world's countries and is celebrated by an increasing number of non-Christians. While the birth year of Jesus is estimated among modern historians to have been between 7 and 2 BC, the precise month and day of his birth are unknown.

The authors of this book are not theologians. We didn't set out to look at Christmas as a cultural or religious phenomenon as there are many excellent writings that cover those complex dimensions of the festival. Our aim is to examine the *natural history* of Christmastide, showing how plants, animals and the environment feature strongly in the celebration. Where we touch upon religion or culture it is with the natural world as our emphasis.

Christmas is an ancient and complex palimpsest and we are reading traces of traditions written and re-written over centuries. In some cases we're following clues to beliefs born far back in history; in others we're uncovering more recent but equally surprising threads to determine something of the shape of the evolving celebrations.

A palimpsest is a manuscript or writing surface that has been used, reused, erased, or altered while retaining traces or ghosts of its earlier content. It is a useful way of describing how people experience Christmastide, that is, as a layering of present experiences over faded pasts. How animals, plants and the natural world feature in both present Christmases and in the 'faded pasts' are the subject of this book. We refine that further to take as our focus the specific customs and rituals of Britain, although many of these have origins way beyond our shores.

These customs are similarly influenced by geographical region within Britain and by social and economic context. Traditions and the processes of celebrating Christmastide differ from peasant to Lord; Northumbrian farmer to London shopkeeper; Scottish crofter to Westminster banker. The source material for these customs is 4000 years of history, pre-Christian belief and post-Christian celebration which coalesce around the rituals. Remembering always that it is the more affluent and socially powerful whose histories are most directly recorded.

Explanations and influences for the origins and trajectory of our traditions jostle and compete. We've aimed to locate the most compelling accounts but much remains in dispute. That continued sense of discovery makes this exploration all the more seductive – and frustrating – and thrilling. The natural history of Christmas is a story continuing to unfold.

THE BASICS...

The year and date of Jesus' birth

One hundred years ago the herald of the Festive Season was Stir-up Sunday, on the last weekend before Advent, when cooks mixed ingredients for the Christmas pudding. This originates from a custom of medieval England that the "pudding should be made on the 25th Sunday after Trinity, that it be prepared with 13 ingredients to represent Christ and the 12 apostles, and that every family member stir it in turn from east to west to honour the Magi and their supposed journey

In the middle of a cold, leafless and lifeless winter, the idea of the returning sun was vitally important to our ancestors.

in that direction". Whatever marks the beginning of your personal countdown today, the awkward truth is that the dating of Christmastide is largely a muddle.

Today we take it for granted that Jesus was born on December 25th but we actually have no firm historical confirmation of this date. There are no written records of the event and, as early Christians didn't celebrate the anniversary, it was many centuries before anyone thought about determining when it actually took place.

One of the problems of fixing a birth-date is that 2000 years ago, there was no single global calendar. Today, on Christmas Day, it is December 25th all around the world; with the slight hiccough of the International Date Line, we share one measurement system. But it wasn't always so simple. Humans have tried to measure the passing of years for millennia and consistently made errors along the way. Early attempts were based on the lunar cycle, making each year about eight weeks too short. When this mistake was finally realised extra days were added to the year, but not enough were tacked on. So with each passing year the seasons and the calendar progressed at different tempos becoming ever further out of synch. Spring,

for example, appeared to come slightly earlier every year. Meanwhile, while the Romans were trying hard to get the calendar right, traditionalists further East still followed the earlier lunar system and soon the people around the Mediterranean were living by entirely different diaries. All was very confused.

Although a reliable year-measuring system was devised around the time Jesus was born, it didn't come into general use until much later. And, importantly, for most people knowing the date was an irrelevance as they couldn't read it or write it. It was knowing the day of the week which was necessary to the common-person's life.

AD/BC

At school we all learn the dating suffixes AD and BC, signifying events after or before the birth of Christ. But this system wasn't adopted until the year 525 AD. More than 500 years after the pivotal event. Incidentally there is no year 'nought', as the concept of 'zero' didn't exist in the Roman world. Counting goes from 1 BC straight to 1 AD, leapfrogging the supposed birth year completely.

The system of enumerating years we still use today was the brainchild of a Scythian (modern day Bulgaria and Romania) monk called Dionysius Exiguus, otherwise known as Dennis the Short. He was working as part of Rome's impressive administrative machine, a system that needed to standardise dates for reasons of census and economics. Dennis worked backwards from his own time to attempt to devise a calendar for the Empire – and this calendar required the pinpointing of Jesus' birth. To undertake these calculations he used peripheral clues such as the known dates of Rome's rulers but things became especially complicated when he accidentally failed to include one! Caesar Augustus was completely forgotten, making the reckoning at least 4 years out. Eventually Dennis came up with a dating method that is still being used 1500 years later. Only it's incorrect. Almost certainly.

History & Scripture

There are very few historical facts to help unravel the dating of the birth of Jesus, consequently it's tempting to look at the New Testament to help solve the conundrum but, sadly, it offers little uncontroversial help.

The famous census that took Joseph and Mary to Bethlehem isn't supported by the impressively accurate Roman records. The only census that took place around that time applied exclusively to Roman citizens, (local Judeans didn't usually have sufficient income to warrant taxation - the prime motivation for a head-count of the populace). The Gospels say that the event took place when Cyrenius was Governor of nearby Syria and we know for certain that he didn't take up that post until 6 AD.

There is one more clue that strongly suggests that we have the dating muddled. The Nativity story's greatest villain is without doubt King Herod, his slaughter of the Innocents is infamous. The massacre took place when Herod heard that a new 'King of the Jews' had been born. Frightened by the prospect of being usurped he ordered the murder of all baby boys under the age of 2 years old. Herod died, in Jericho, in 4 BC. So already the Gospel facts are in direct conflict, even allowing for unintentional mistakes that crop up in all stories of antiquity

There isn't enough evidence for us to guess with any accuracy the year of Jesus' birth, it seems that it was somewhere between 7 BC and 2 AD but that's far from proven.

With nothing else to go on the Romans, and then the modern world, quietly adopted the dating created by Dennis the Short.

THE DATE
A return of the sun

As festivals are an intrinsic part of most belief-systems, it was essential for Christianity that there should be a date to commemorate the birth of Jesus, so the early church had to settle upon one. The search was for the most worthy.

For thousands of years, cultures in the northern hemisphere have marked the winter solstice, the shortest day of the year. China had its Dongzhi festival, the Hopi Indians of south-west America celebrated Soyal, while Yalda was the biggest event in ancient Persia (modern Iran). In Britain the mid-winter solstice was celebrated for centuries before Christianity arrived.

These festivities had one thing in common, they all welcomed the return of the sun and the promise of renewal it bestowed. After the gloom of a long cold winter, days slowly became longer and warmer, crops once again started to appear and farm animals gave birth. The solstice signalled growth, new life and hope. It's hard to imagine a better symbolic time at which to situate the birth date of a religion.

Emperor Aurelian ruled the Roman world for just six years, but played an important part in the Christmas story. He was a sun worshipper and in 274 AD Aurelian proclaimed an official day of worship called *Dies Natalis Solis Invicti*, "Birthday of the Unconquered Sun".

That day was December 25th.

Saturnalia – a perfect disguise

Saturnalia is believed to originate as a celebration to mark the end of a successful annual harvest, it takes its name from Saturn, the god of harvest and time. Records show that as the Roman Empire became more powerful, the festival evolved into an orgy of food, wine and song. In a contemporary poem, written by Lucian of Samosata, Saturn himself said "during my week the serious is barred; no business allowed. Drinking and being drunk, noise and games and dice, appointing of kings and feasting of slaves, singing naked, clapping of tremulous hands, an occasional ducking of corked faces in icy water,--such are the functions over which I preside"

The choice of December to celebrate Jesus' birth offered one tempting, very practical benefit. The Romans themselves already had a well established mid-winter Festival known as *Saturnalia*; originally it coincided with the shortest day, when they gave thanks to the god Saturn for the returning light. But over the centuries it slowly evolved into a hedonistic week-long celebration in which everyone ate and drank to excess. Saturnalia was the noisiest shindig of the Roman world and everything else stopped for the festivities. At this time Christianity was still a minority movement and its followers were subject to persecution. Emperors such as Nero executed Christians so most were subtle about their worship. However devotees still wanted to mark feast days. There could be no better place to hide a forbidden celebration than during a time when the whole of the known world was having one huge party. With just a little discretion, the first celebrations of Christmas would have passed unnoticed.

Saturnalia involved eating and drinking, role playing and dressing in ornate costume. The highlight of the festivities was a day known as the *Sigillaria* when friends and family exchanged gifts. Children were given toys and adults often received more expensive presents. Sigillaria fell on December 23rd and most scholars accept that this is the origin of our own gift giving at Christmas.

Saturnalia was slowly abandoned and disappeared completely around the beginning of the 4th Century AD. That's just the time when Emperor Constantine issued a decree that finally allowed Christians to practice their faith freely and without persecution. At last Christmas could be celebrated openly, fixed forever on December 25th.

Light in the darkness

Almost all animals are influenced by the changing of the seasons, some species migrate, others hibernate, many go through a transformation of fur colour or moult their feathers and even dietary preferences shift. Humans are similarly influenced. In recent years scientists have identified a cyclical condition that causes many people to suffer from depression. Popular culture has known about the malady for centuries but now it has an official name 'seasonal affective disorder' or SAD for short. It can occasionally occur in summer but mainly SAD shows itself in the short winter days. Humans evolved outdoors in tropical Africa and we are diurnal, a species that is active during the day - so light is part of our evolution. Scientists have long understood that we need sunshine both psychologically and physiologically. That's not a problem in summer but winters are a challenge, particularly as our ancestors inexorably moved away from the tropics where day length remains at 12 hours all year round. It's a basic law of geography that winters get darker as we move away from the Equator. Northern temperate zones in mid December have days that are just 8 hours long and even those are often cloudy and wet. Entire weeks can pass without the sun once appearing and medicine now recognises that this can make us feel very low indeed.

In northern Europe alone an estimated 12 million people suffer from SAD today. Symptoms include depressed energy levels, lack of concentration and decreased appetite. Sufferers report feeling lethargic and pessimistic about life, which is why the feeling is often known as the 'winter blues'.

In addition to boosting our levels of Vitamin D, research from Edinburgh University suggests that exposure to average levels of sunlight cuts down the risk of heart attacks and strokes and helps lower blood pressure. Today SAD, when it is diagnosed, is treated with light therapy

or the use of the hormone melatonin. But 2000 years ago management was very different.

As winter solstice celebrations cropped up in unconnected places around the northern hemisphere many anthropologists believe is it likely that our ancestors instinctively understood that they needed something to raise their spirits at this dismal time. A hearty, red-blooded week-long festival of indulgence could provide an excellent tonic.

Well, it is Christmas...

Behaviourists accept that it is these 'winter blues' that prompt humans into excess at Christmas. In cold weather all animals require more food to keep warm, for most 21st Century humans that is now irrelevant as most of us don't live or work out in the elements. Our living conditions may have changed but, biologically, we are identical to humans of 40,000 years ago. At an instinctive level we still understand that certain foods help us feel better at the gloomiest time of the year. When the weather becomes harsh humans subconsciously seek out two basic food groups, sugar and fat. That's why, at Christmas, we load ourselves with too much cake, trifle, roast ham and pudding. Very few people, when looking for comfort-

A single cocoa pod contains between 20 and 50 beans, enough to make a small bar of chocolate.

food, reach for celery and carrots. But while our ancestors struggled to find enough of these rich foods; pure sugar is rare in the natural world and fat requires a hunting expedition, modern life makes them readily available. Deep-seated instincts influence what we want to eat, and we've discovered that sugary, rich treats help us feel better – in the short-term. Treats like chocolate…

Chocolate

The scientific term for chocolate is *Theobroma cacao*, we hold it in such high esteem that we named it 'food of the Gods.' Chocolate comes from the seeds of a small evergreen tree originally found in Central America. Humans have been harvesting the seeds for at least 3000 years, they used them to make fermented drinks and crushed them to add to smoking tobacco. The ancients believed that cocao seeds boosted intelligence, energized the body and acted as an aphrodisiac. The Spanish conquistadors reported that Emperor Moctezuma II drank 50 cups of chocolate every day.

The name we use today comes from the Aztec word *xocolat*, meaning bitter water. Unsweetened chocolate is an acquired taste, it was enjoyed 1000 years ago but is not so appealing to a modern palate. Jose de Acosta, a 16th Century Spanish missionary, wrote that the chocolate drink was 'loathsome to such as are not acquainted with it, having a scum or froth that is [a] very unpleasant taste'. However it was so highly regarded by the locals that the Spanish took it home and a chocolate drink was given to King Phillip II in 1544.

Chocolate treats have become an intrinsic part of Christmas celebrations.

13

The first recorded commercial chocolate shipment arrived in Europe in 1585. At this time cocoa seeds could be collected only from the wild state and shipped across the Atlantic. As a result chocolate was extremely expensive and unaffordable for most people, it was therefore highly fashionable, the 'bitter water' being made more palatable by the addition of honey or sugar. Little changed with the brew until the end of the 17ᵗʰ Century when Hans Sloane (he of the London Square and British Museum) decided that the new drink was 'nauseous' and set out to improve it. Sloane was a true Renaissance man; he was an entrepreneur, collector of curiosities and Royal Physician to Queen Ann, George I and George II. Using good scientific methods he carried out exhaustive experiments before coming up with a successful cocoa recipe in 1689. It involved crushing the beans and boiling them slowly in milk, then adding sugar. The resulting drink was unlike anything tasted before and was an instant hit. The recipe was soon bought by an apothecary and marketed as "Sir Hans Sloane's Milk Chocolate". In the 19ᵗʰ Century the still-secret formula was sold again, this time to a Birmingham tea merchant – by the name of John Cadbury.

Meanwhile in 1828 a Dutchman called van Houten was busy working out a method of processing the seeds to remove the fat, known as cocoa butter, leaving just cocoa powder. He mixed the dark brown powder with sugar and a few additives to remove the bitter taste, this concoction then solidified and chocolate was no longer a drink. A few years later milk was added for the first time and the modern chocolate bar was born. Christmas would never be quite the same again.

We eat more chocolate at Christmas than any other time of the year, exceeding even Easter with all of its chocolate eggs. It comes in selection boxes, foil-wrapped and hanging on the tree, in the shape of oranges and nestled in expensive Belgian presentation packs. Chocolate is consumed partly because it features fat and sugar, the critical food groups that we instinctively crave in-hostile weather, but also because it contains small traces of 'feel good' chemicals such as caffeine that help banish the 'winter blues'.

We now know that a key component of chocolate is *phenylethylamine*, a naturally occurring plant-based compound that stimulates the brain's pleasure centres and produces a sense of excitable well-being. Its effects last only a few minutes but, as can be confirmed by millions of chocoholics, are very agreeable. Incidentally phenylethylamine belongs to the same chemical family as the recreational drug Ecstasy, and the effects, though dilute, are not dissimilar. It's a good idea to remember that small biological detail when children become exuberant after indulging in too much Christmas chocolate.

Alcoholic treats

Alcohol has been part of human culture for at least 10,000 years. Today we think of it as a product of modern fermentation and distillation processes but it cropped up spontaneously long ago in nature.

Alcoholic drinks are based on *ethanol*, a chemical derived from living plants. Plants contain natural sugars such as glucose and sucrose and, under certain circumstances,

these will ferment slowly and be converted into ethanol. In warm weather a bowl of ripe pears will decay and, amongst other things, produce alcohol. A very long time ago our ancestors noticed the after-effects of eating such foods and soon learned to reproduce them intentionally.

Hops are fast-growing perennial climbers, a little like vines. They require good soil and thrive on south facing slopes that receive plenty of sunshine.

Mead was almost certainly the first man-made alcoholic drink, simply because it's the easiest to produce. Mead is fermented honey, a food that obviously contains plenty of sugar. At its most basic mead can be made by mixing honey and water in a jar and leaving it somewhere warm to process. Six weeks later out pours a very strong tipple. Mead was simultaneously discovered in Europe, Asia and Africa, all places with honey bees. There were countless variations created by adding fruit, spices, herbs and whatever could be found locally.

Shortly after the invention of mead, beer

Barley is a member of the grass family and was one of the first grain crops to be farmed by humans. The technique was perfected in Mesopotamia around 10,000 years ago. Barley meal was used to make flat bread and gruel, it was also the basis of beer, one of the world's first alcoholic drinks.

was discovered. At first it simply involved the fermentation of barley with just as many variations and additions as mead. This bore little resemblance to the modern drink as it lacked one vital ingredient – hops. These are the female flowers of the hop tree that originated in China. The first reference to their use in beer dates back to 822 AD, but they weren't included regularly until much later. Beer with hops didn't arrive in Britain until around 1400 AD, it was imported from the Netherlands where it had been made. It was to be more than 100 years before we started to grow hops here and included the flowers in our own brewing. Hops gave barley beer the bitter quality that defines the taste today.

Roman grapes were smaller and less hardy than the strains used for wine in the 21st Century.

Wine emerged from warmer countries where grapes could thrive. The fruit seems to have evolved somewhere near Turkey but was quickly cultivated and introduced to most of the Mediterranean basin. At first they were probably grown only for food but with their high sugar content grapes were ideally suited to the production of alcohol. The Romans first carried wine to our shores. It was culturally so important to the Empire that its armies also brought living vines out into the Provinces so that they could grow grapes in the new lands and establish their own wineries. This wasn't a hugely successful enterprise as 2000 years ago Roman grape varieties, perfectly suited to the Italian climate, didn't do well in our cold and wet weather. Much of the wine used to celebrate Saturnalia's mid-winter solstice was imported from countries like Italy and Spain – not unlike today!

Mulled Wine

Mulled wine is a Christmas drink of spiced, generally red, wine. It is served hot and is traditionally drunk during winter.

Bequeathed to Britain by the Romans, ordinary legionnaires couldn't afford the best wine, so they worked hard to improve less-than-perfect drinks by adding a little something extra. A flagon of wine was very acceptable in the summer but didn't help keep out the cold of a British winter storm, particularly when you were a native of Southern Italy – mulled wine to the rescue! Traditionally the wine was heated by plunging in a red-hot poker that had just been taken from the fire. This raised the temperature and added a scalded, smoking flavour.

Over the years mulled wine recipes have changed and slowly become more exotic. Today most feature cinnamon, cloves and nutmeg - spices that were unknown in Britain until the 17th Century.

Mulled wine was popular in Victorian England. One key recipe was Smoking Bishop. It appears in Dickens' story, *A Christmas Carol.*

Smoking Bishop includes port, red wine, Seville oranges or lemons, sugar and spices. The fruit was roasted to caramelise it and the ingredients then warmed together. The name is derived from the shape of the traditional bowl used to heat the brew, shaped like a bishop's mitre. It was served in universities and medieval guildhalls.

The famous German version of mulled wine is called *Glühwein* (meaning, "glow-wine," from the hot irons once used for mulling). It is usually made from red wine, warmed and infused with cinnamon, cloves, citrus, star aniseed, sugar and sometimes vanilla. Glühwein is offered throughout Christmastide.

A Victorian Mulled Wine Recipe
From *Mrs Beeton's Book of Household Management*
By Isabella Beeton. 1869 Edition

"In making preparations like the above, it is very difficult to give the exact proportions of ingredients like sugar and spice, as what quantity might suit one person would be to another quite distasteful. Boil the spice in the water until the flavour is extracted, then add the wine and sugar, and bring the whole to the boiling-point, then serve with strips of crisp dry toast, or with biscuits. The spices usually used for mulled wine are cloves, grated nutmeg, and cinnamon or mace. Any kind of wine may be mulled, but port and claret are those usually selected for the purpose; and the latter requires a very large proportion of sugar. The vessel that the wine is boiled in must be delicately cleaned, and should be kept exclusively for the purpose. Small tin warmers may be purchased for a trifle, which are more suitable than saucepans, as, if the latter are not scrupulously clean; they spoil the wine, by imparting to it a very disagreeable flavour. These warmers should be used for no other purpose."

Punch

In 1632 a new drink appears in British literature – punch. From the Hindi word *panch* meaning five, punch was a drink originally made with five ingredients - tea, alcohol, sugar, lemon and spices – though the exact mix varied. The recipe was brought to England by employees of the British East India Company. Sailors, transporting goods to and from India, were the first to adopt the drink. In those times when at sea each sailor was entitled to 10 pints of beer a day but in the heat of the tropics their supply quickly spoiled. By using it to produce punch, the taste of soured beer was masked by the other ingredients and they could still enjoy their daily ration. The formula was very elastic and the list of ingredients was followed only loosely. One 1668 punch recipe includes a lump of ambergris, clotted whale cholesterol, to add fragrance. Modern punch makers tend to omit this variation.

The pre-existing British version of punch was 'wassail' – wassail is both a drink and a ritual. The tradition of wassailing was popular at Christmastime amongst the cider-producing counties of Britain. Wassailing, an ancient southern English drinking ritual, was intended to ensure a good cider apple harvest the following year. It was customary on Twelfth Night for revellers to visit orchards and the houses of friends and relatives to wish them well and to ensure the fertility of the next year's crop. In return they would be offered wassail the drink - mulled beer or mead with sugar, ale, ginger, nutmeg and cinnamon added. The brew would be would be heated in a bowl, and topped with slices of toast as sops. A sop is a piece of toast or bread that is dipped into a liquid foodstuff before being eaten. In medieval times sops were very familiar. They were served with wine, beer, soup or broth. The words "soup" and "sop" sharing a common root.

Back on dry land in Britain, the sailors' punch gained a wider popularity. The alcoholic aspect of punch could be wine, sherry, cider or beer, depending on the available budget. But then, from the Caribbean, the rum trade started to popularise a new spirit. The two were put together and the rum punch was born. Rum is made by distilling molasses, a by-product of sugar production from cane. It wasn't discovered until the 17th Century when sugar production was well established in the Caribbean. It was relatively cheap to produce, although the early attempts were a little coarse. Rum was first described in 1651 by John Ligon, an Englishman living in Barbados, he called it "a hot, hellish, and terrible liquor". But when the techniques were refined rum was enthusiastically received by Europeans.

Incidentally, food historians believe that the introduction of punch from India lead directly to the invention of cocktails, another Christmas favourite.

Full of Christmas Spirit

Spirits are a much later invention than wine as they require more technical knowledge and specialised equipment to produce than simple fermentation. Distillation is a method of separating mixtures based on the differences in volatility of components in a boiling liquid mixture. The process of distilling seems to have been invented in Egypt around the time of the Nativity. But early experimenters were diligently exploring scientific principles and focused on water – distilling to remove impurities, such as salt from seawater. It was several hundred years before the technique was adapted to produce a more commercial product. Distillation of already fermented solutions was used to produce beverages with a higher alcohol content. The first distilling pioneers simply boiled wine, turning it into steam and then condensing it onto a cold surface so that the steam reformed into water. It's exactly the same process that makes windows steam up in a shower room. Distilling concentrates the alcohol levels and produces a much more potent drink.

By the 13th Century distillation was a black art, a skilled and secretive process known to an initiated few. Practitioners used wheat, plums and juniper berries, amongst many other plantstuffs, as the basis for their new exotic brews. In those days spirits were used mainly for medicinal purposes, they were too valuable to drink for simple enjoyment. It wasn't until the 16th Century that spirits made any cultural impact. The turning point was the production of Hieronymus Brunschweig's *Vertuose Boke of Distillation*, this best-seller introduced the art of spirit-making to a much wider world. Brunschweig was a German doctor with a fascination for all things new and technological, he based the text on his own experiments and his book clearly explained the apparatus, method and ingredients need for distillation. His systems were practical, straightforward and efficient. They worked well and so stills were set up around Europe and soon we had the brandy (from the Dutch *brandewijn,* meaning burnt wine) and whisky (from the Gaelic *uisce beatha*, meaning 'water of life') that form the heart of our Christmas spirit consumption.

Frankincense (right) and myrrh were highly valued commodities 2000 years ago. Even today they fetch relatively high prices.

The Wise Men and Epiphany

No Nursery School Christmas play could be complete without the appearance of the three wise men who, according to the Gospel of Matthew, found baby Jesus by "following" a star, which thus traditionally became known as the Star of Bethlehem. Many theories have been proposed as to what this phenomenon refers, since stars do not visibly move and therefore cannot be followed. It has been suggested that they might actually have followed a planet, which could be mistaken as a star, as it slowly moved across the sky.

In Christian liturgy, the meeting of the wise men and Jesus marks Epiphany – the revelation of Jesus as divine. The date set for this is January 6th, also, in the modern calendar, Twelfth Night. This keystone of the Christmas story is full of mystery and uncertainty. The Bible does not actually confirm for us how many wise men visited Bethlehem carrying gifts. The word used for the visitors is 'magi' (Greek) and 'magi' doesn't mean 'kings' as the Christmas carol suggests, rather, a closer translation would be 'astrologers'. As the word magi is plural, it's reasonable to assume that there was more than one visitor but nowhere in the scriptures does it state a number. We cannot be certain of the names of the wise men or the lands from which they journeyed. The phrase 'from the east', or more literally 'from the rising (of the sun)', is the only information Matthew's Gospel gives about the region from which they visited. Fortunately, more clarity exists about the gifts they brought with them.

*Camels and donkeys may appear on Christmas cards and Nativity
tableaux but they don't feature in the Biblical account.*

Gold, Frankincense and Myrrh

Gold is the icon of wealth, for much of recorded human history it has been of huge financial and symbolic value. But the popularity of frankincense and myrrh in the west has slipped a little over the last 2000 years other than at Christmastime when reference to them is frequent.

Myrrh and frankincense are dried resins made from tree sap. They are harvested by gouging the tree's bark and, later, collecting the thick, sticky sap that oozes out. This dries into rock-hard pieces that resemble dirty fragments of coloured glass. These are then ground very finely and added to oil. Both resins are exquisitely perfumed and were used to mask unwanted odours and for incense burning.

Frankincense comes from the *boswellia* tree which is native to East Africa, a family of trees renowned for its ability to grow in the rockiest and most inhospitable of deserts. Frankincense resin has been traded for at least 5000 years; nowadays it is still used as a spicy perfume but is also eaten in small doses to aid digestion and can be easily bought in most markets in the Middle East.

Myrrh is produced by the *commiphora* tree found in the Horn of Africa and the Arabian peninsula. It has always been much more valuable than frankincense because it was believed to have near magical medicinal properties. At times myrrh was, weight for weight, as expensive as gold. Traditionally myrrh was used as an antiseptic in wounds and as a pain-reliever. Ancient Egyptians used it as part of their embalming processes when preparing mummies and eastern medicine recommends myrrh as a way of strengthening the heart, liver and blood. In the west we use it on a daily basis as a hidden ingredient in toothpastes, mouthwashes and as an additive to liniments designed to treat muscle injuries.

The Nativity Scene

In primary schools, echoing village halls and brightly-lit shopping malls around the land, cosy pre-Christmas Nativity scenes herald the approach of Christmastide. They show tableaux of Joseph, Mary and baby Jesus in a stable surrounded by a host of farm animals being visited by three wise men and a group of shepherds. There might be a donkey, camel, sheep, goat, dog or an ox transfixed on the new-born child. Each scene has its own particular menagerie.

But what do the Gospels tell us about the species that were actually present at the time? Only two, Luke and Matthew, refer to the birth of Jesus, but not a single farm animal is mentioned in either account – and neither is a stable. Luke tells us that an angel appeared to a group of shepherds, saying that Christ had been born in Bethlehem and that he had a message of good news for all people, namely that "Today in the town of David a Saviour has been born to you; he is the Messiah, the Lord. This will be a sign to you: You will find a baby wrapped in cloths and lying in a manger."

The presence of the shepherds and the reference to the manger invites us to imagine a pastoral scene. The animal figures we expect to see, and those depicted in art and in countless nativity scenes, have all been added over the centuries by people interpreting and elaborating the Gospels.

Christian art offers us the Annunciation to the shepherds – in which the Angels deliver news of the birth of Jesus, and the Adoration of the shepherds and the Magi – in which they visit baby Jesus, as frequent depictions. The addition of animals to the scant scriptural information underpinning these scenes has, over time, helped artists to clarify their subjects. A baby placed in a wooden crib-like structure becomes a manger by the addition of on-looking animals, we know men in the hills are shepherds by adding sheep and dogs to the scene, or that men carrying gifts come from the East by placing them on camels. These details have also helped to add atmosphere and romance. The fact that the animals seem to look on the child with wonder adds to the sense of holiness and majesty.

Similarly, many depictions of Mary and Joseph arriving in Bethlehem include a donkey. But this too is not mentioned in the Gospels.

Deck the Halls ...

Wily conquerors with unfamiliar belief systems frequently adopt and adapt the existing customs of their newly subjugated cultures, absorbing them into the rituals of the new order to make the transition appear less radical and ease opposition. In this way, customs and practices remain but their interpretation may shift. This evolution of tradition allows each generation to follow the actions of their ancestors - to do what parents and grandparents did - not because of any edict but because the familiarity generates a kind of security. The repetition of much-loved childhood traditions provides a sense of continuity, it makes us feel content and safe. Some traditions, particularly those surrounding significant festivals, date back much further than we imagine. These habits include our choice of Christmas decorations.

Only the female holly produces berries. In the early winter the berries are very hard and are often not eaten by birds until the New Year when frost has made them a little softer. Berried holly was one of the few colourful plants visible in mid-December.

Holly

Every year holly is woven into wreaths, spiked into Christmas puddings and has a starring role on Christmas cards. Yet it has nothing to do with the Christmas story and there's no mention of it anywhere in Bethlehem - the use of mid-winter holly comes, as we shall see, from a much more ancient time.

Many pagan cultures were Animistic, that is, they held a belief that a plethora of supernatural spirits lived in water, rocks, plants and animals. The spirits could be bad or good and must be appeased if death and disaster were to be avoided. In this belief system evergreen plants were potent. As they were healthy and vibrant all year round, they were seen to house the most dominant spirits, beings who could overcome even the destructive and paralysing power of winter. The Druids believed that part of the sun's power dwelt inside holly leaves. This wasn't important in the summer months when there was plenty of sunlight available but it became critical in colder times. The last rays of summer, held in the spiky green leaves, must be protected at all costs. It was believed that if a forest lost its holly, there would be no sun to come back in the spring. Cutting down a holly tree was considered to bring the worst kind of bad luck down on the axe-bearer.

Sprigs of holly were brought indoors in winter, to keep the sun safe. Our ancestors needed to ensure that good weather would return and bring with it food and warmth. When deciduous trees were lifeless and leafless, holly boughs were given to friends as symbols of good fortune, long life and a fertile future. Holly bushes became important portents and were often planted close to houses, as people believed that the trees' sun spirits would protect the home from witches and other malevolent forest forces. These beliefs had no specific connection with Christmas and predate the festival by thousands of years. Until quite recently the plant was called by its Old English name *hole*, for a reason we don't yet understand the spelling changed in the Middle Ages to something more familiar, but it still contained only one 'l'. The plant became known as the 'holy tree'. That, combined with the long established mid-winter tradition of keeping sprigs indoors, guaranteed the holly's place in our Christmas life.

Ivy

In temperate zones any plant that stays green all winter was revered by our ancestors and was often granted special status. Ancient Greece and Rome were pantheistic societies; they worshipped many gods each with their own areas of authority. Some associations were curiously impenetrable - such as Deverra, the goddess of brooms or Summanus, the God of nocturnal thunder.

Portrayed here by Caravaggio, Bacchus was believed to be the offspring of a God and a human. His father was Jupiter and his mother Semele, daughter of the king of Thebes. He was one of Rome's most important deities and took his place on Dei Consentes – the Council of Gods.

There was a deity for every occasion and each was associated with specific plants and animals that were deliberately used to identify him or her in murals and statues. The immediate importance of each God depended on the activity or season. During Saturnalia, the proto-Christmas mid-winter festival, one deity ruled supreme – Bacchus (in Greek mythology he was called Dionysus), the god of wine and ecstasy. His particular plant totem was ivy and he was often portrayed with a wreath around his head in paintings. The Romans were devoted to their deities for centuries but as the early piety faded, the gods became less important. Towards the end of its popularity, Saturnalia had become an excuse for over-indulgence, and the drink of choice was wine.

Roman wine could be fierce, containing much more alcohol than the modern equivalent. The drink produced for the hoi-polloi was often mixed with herbs, spices and even sea-water, only the rich could afford more refined products. Poor wine was drunk when it was still young and often high in tannins and other impurities, the compounds that cause hangovers. First-

hand contemporary reports from party guests 2000 years ago tell us that raucous Romans suffered terribly the morning after hard drinking sessions. Luckily they all knew that the unpleasant effects of wine could be considerably reduced by appealing to its controlling deity, Bacchus. The accepted way to pay homage to him was to drink from a goblet carved from a single ivy stem, acknowledging Bacchus' part in producing the drink and the occasion. If an ivy goblet wasn't available revellers simply wrapped a little ivy around the wine cup and hoped that Bacchus would offer protection against the dire consequences of over consumption.

Sadly, this is more fanciful than factual. Surprisingly, the partying Romans didn't rumble the myth. With uncharacteristically faulty logic, they believed that if they didn't carry out the Bacchus ritual, then their hangovers would simply have been even worse. Ivy-protected drinking was widespread and does help explain why people brought ivy into houses for the mid-winter celebrations. Something we've been doing ever since despite the hangover's persistence!

Mistletoe

Reverence toward mistletoe is ancient. It was sacred to the Norse, the Celtic Druids and the North American Indians. Druid priests believed it had magical properties, particularly when growing on an oak tree. They used a golden sickle to cut mistletoe branches which had to be caught mid-air before they touched the ground and lost their potency. Sprigs were then distributed to people for protection against evil and to ensure fertility.

Mistletoe is a powerful symbol of peace. This connection also has its origin in Druidic lore which insists that whenever enemies met under the mistletoe in the forest, they must lay down their arms and observe a truce until the next day.

The supernatural power of mistletoe is

witnessed in the Norse legend of Goddess Frigga and her son Balder. Frigga was the Goddess of Love and Balder was the God of the Summer Sun. Once, while sleeping, Balder foresaw his own death. When he told his mother about the dream, Frigga feared not only for the life of her son but also for all life on Earth because she knew that without Balder and the Summer Sun, everything would end. She appealed to the Earth's elements: air, water, fire and earth, and asked all creatures of each element to promise that they would never bring harm to her son. They gave their word and she was promised the safety of her son by every animal and plant under and above the Earth. However, Loki, the God of Evil, was aware that there was one plant that Frigga had overlooked.

It grew neither on or over the earth, but on oak trees. Loki made an arrow and placed a sprig of sharpened mistletoe at its tip. He then beguiled Hoder, the blind brother of Balder and the God of Winter, to have him shoot this arrow at Balder.

Balder died and immediately the world turned cold. For the next three days, every creature tried to bring Balder back to life without success. The mistletoe's white berries were formed from Frigga's tears of mourning. However, some versions of the story of Balder's death end more happily. They tell that when Frigga placed these berries upon Balder's breast, he came to life again. And so, Frigga praised the mistletoe as a symbol of love and of peace, and she promised that, ever afterwards, whoever stood beneath this plant would be offered a kiss and forever protected.

The spirit of the Norse myth – Frigga's love conquering death with the aid of mistletoe - resounds with the Christian idea of belief overcoming death. Mistletoe as an emblem

Little is known about the Druids, as they left few written records. The only hard facts come from contemporary Roman historians. Druids were Celtic mystics, they probably occupied the same social position as shamen in other tribal cultures.

of love thus finds a sympathetic placement in the Christmastide celebrations.

Celtic Druids saw magic in the mistletoe as it remained vibrant in winter when other plants appeared dead. In this way it again became connected to the concept of eternal life. Cut sprigs were thought to have restorative powers that helped fight disease; its Celtic name meant 'all-heal'. Mistletoe became a symbol of life and fertility, women often sowed a little into the hem of their dresses to ensure a fecund future.

Mistletoe is used as a Christmas decoration throughout Europe and America, though such use was rarely documented until the 18th Century. In cultures across ancient Europe, mistletoe was seen as a representation of divine male essence, of romance and fertility. When Christianity became widespread after the 3rd Century AD, the sacred or mystical respect for the mistletoe plant was integrated into the new religion. Leading to the widespread custom of kissing under the mistletoe during the Christmas season. The earliest documented case of this dates from 16th Century England.

Apparently rootless and growing high amongst the branches of lime and silver birch trees, mistletoe was like no other plant in the forests that once blanketed Europe. Even today mistletoe is unique in the woodland because of its unusual parasitic habits. Unlike other plants, as Frigga discovered, mistletoe doesn't touch the earth, it appears to grow out of the air and is metaphorically between worlds. Some cultures maintained that the plant was seeded by lightning, emerging on the part of a tree that had been directly hit. That is believed to be one of the reasons why we brought it into our houses in the autumn, the season when storms are at their worst in the northern hemisphere. Until recently houses were made of wood and lightning strikes were to be dreaded. People understood (wrongly) that lightning never strikes twice in the same spot, hence bringing mistletoe into a house kept it safe

The scientific name of the mistle thrush is Turdus viscivorus. Viscivorus means mistletoe-eater.

Many of our most enduring Christmas traditions emerge from ancient Norse mythology.

in autumn, they digest the soft flesh of the berries but the hard seeds inside pass through the digestive system and emerge a while later in the birds' droppings. As the birds flit amongst the trees, the seeds are deposited complete with fertiliser on a completely new host where they can take root. Incidentally the plant's name comes from two Anglo-Saxon words, *mistel* meaning 'dung' and *tan* meaning 'twig'. As our ancestors called the birds *misteltan,* it's clear they'd already worked out the main seed dispersal mechanism.

Blackcaps have a slightly different distribution system. They don't swallow the entire berry, they eat just the soft flesh then push the seed out of the side of their beaks and wipe it onto a suitable branch. Each seed is coated with a sticky material called *viscin*. The viscin soon hardens and attaches the seed firmly to its future host, where it germinates and its *haustorium* (the mistletoe's 'root' system through which it absorbs water and nutrients) penetrates the sound bark.

As ancient peoples had to wait for the invention of microscopes to discover the haustorium, our pragmatic ancestors simply assumed that the plant was supernatural. Mistletoe grows on many deciduous trees but it thrives particularly on apple.

in wild weather. Mistletoe would hang over doorways, in cowsheds and over cradles to make the occupants safe.

The biological reality of the plant is no less fascinating than the legends, like many other plants mistletoe is distributed by birds. The main culprits are blackcap and mistle thrush, which is a shortened form of mistletoe thrush. The plants' white berries can cause unpleasant effects when eaten by humans but are perfectly palatable to birds. Mistle thrushes eat them by the hundreds

Yule Log

In Norway and Sweden Christmas is known as *Jul*, in Finland it is called *Joulua*. In each language the letter J is pronounced as a Y. Our modern word Yule comes directly from ancient Norse **houl** which means wheel, the people from the North believed that the sun was a wheel that changed the seasons. The shortest day was important as it marked the end of one year and the start of another, the beginning of a new cycle as the wheel turned again. The turning point of Yule was one of the most significant sacred events of the calendar and it took place in the month of *juliess*, December.

Coming from a land that experienced extremely short days in mid-winter, Nordic tradition maintained that the sun became dangerously weak for twelve days around the solstice. During this time they burned a large log continuously, this would bring good luck and drive away the evil spirits that thrived whenever there was no sunlight. Heat and light from the fire would overcome the darkness and allow the sun to return for another year.

The Yule log tradition was almost certainly brought to Britain by Viking invaders who first raided Northumberland in 793 AD. Originally the Vikings came in search of treasure but later many moved here to colonise the land, bringing with them new words and customs. As with most Viking practices, remoteness of location meant that the south of England remained largely untouched by the introduced beliefs. It wasn't until the 17th Century that the Yule log emerges in the literature of Britain. The poet and clergyman Robert Herrick, writing from the early 1600s, called the tradition a "Christmas log". The log was brought into a farmhouse by a group of men, who were then given beer by the farmer's wife. The fire used to burn the log was always kindled with a remnant from the log that had been burned in the previous year's festivities. The log's role was to bring prosperity and to protect against evil.

Log burning remains an important part of Scandinavian winter festivals – perhaps this is an echo of the Yule log?

The Yule or Christmas log is connected to other Christmastide traditions such as the ashen faggot - a custom from the West Country. A faggot can be a single log or a bundle of ash sticks. It was bound with nine green lengths of ash bands or 'beams', ideally from the same tree. The faggot was burned in a hearth on Christmas Eve.

The ash tree has a long history of magical associations: perhaps the most important is the *Yggdrasil* of Norse mythology, a tree connecting all nine worlds of their cosmology. The ashen faggot ritual is related to the tradition of wassailing, an ancient southern English drinking ritual originally intended to ensure a good cider apple harvest the following year. Wassail refers both to the salute 'Waes Hail' and to the drink of wassail, a mulled cider.

The wassail ceremony involves singing and toasting the health of orchard trees. The aim is to awaken the cider apple trees and to drive off evil spirits to ensure a good harvest in the autumn. The ceremonies of each wassail vary but they generally all have the same key elements. A wassail King and Queen lead the song or tune from one orchard to the next; the Queen is then lifted into the tree where she places toast soaked in wassail as a gift to the tree spirits. In some counties the youngest boy will act

Today we maintain the Vikings' habit of bringing light indoors during the winter solstice by lighting candles at Christmas.

as a substitute for the Queen and hang the toast in the tree. Then an incantation is frequently recited.

During the wassail party a bundle of bound ash sticks, containing a remnant of the previous year's faggot, is passed around to everyone present and then placed onto the fire. As each binding snaps in the flames, it is toasted with a drink.

When the bundle has fallen loose, each person intending to host the festivities next year takes one of the half-burned sticks and saves it until the following Christmas, when it will go in the centre of their own ashen faggot. This ritual symbolizes the continuity of life. It continues or has been re-established in many villages. To quote from the website of The Harbour Inn in Axmouth:

"The Harbour Inn… dates back to the 12th Century. There is a huge stone fireplace in the main bar where the tradition of making a faggot dates back hundreds of years and still happens to this day. The burning of the ashen faggot takes place every Christmas Eve, when a massive faggot in a hazel twig bundle, some six feet long and three feet wide fills the pub's open fire. The faggot burning is accompanied by verses and carol singing."

The shift from open hearths and an agricultural economy has meant that the popularity of the Yule Log has diminished somewhat, however, the *Bûche de Noël* or Chocolate Log dessert has become a Christmas tradition in Britain. The Chocolate log is a kind of roulade. The bûche is made from a sponge cake, generally baked in a Swiss roll pan, filled with cream or butter cream, rolled to form a cylinder, and coated with chocolate on the outside.

So remember when you next cut a slice of Chocolate Yule Log , you're just keeping faith with an ancient Viking ritual.

CHRISTMAS MENU

There has long been a tendency to eat more meat in winter than at any other time of the year. Hunting is often easier at this time as prey animals frequently become weak through lack of food. There are also biological reasons for this subtle shift in diet, in cold weather we burn more calories to keep warm. But unfortunately this need falls at a time when the supply of available food sources is limited. Eggs, fruit, vegetables, nuts and fungi that are plentiful in other seasons are difficult to find in mid December. In cold weather our ancestors turned to the preserving cupboard, the hunt or simply slaughtered domestic livestock. Over thousands of years humans learned to associate winter with meat, not for cultural reasons but for survival. Even today the centre piece of many Christmas meals remains a roast.

Turkeys

The name of this bird causes confusion, it suggests that they come from the country in Asia Minor while, in fact, they are natives of North America and, as such, were completely unknown in Europe until Columbus' voyage of 1492. Turkeys were once found throughout the New World but over-hunting has now dramatically reduced their range. They usually live in loose groups and, although they are able to fly,

At first early European settlers didn't believe that turkeys were edible - they were not the most conventionally handsome birds and the settlers were deterred by their appearance.

An 18th Century engraving of a turkey by Thomas Bewick.

prefer to spend most of their time on the ground. Even before humans came along, these birds faced a formidable array of predators: wolves, coyotes, mountain lions and bobcats. They were also a favourite meat source for the indigenous Indians. It was probably the native Wampanoag tribe that introduced interloping Europeans to a tasty new meal in the 17th Century, shortly after their arrival in Massachusetts.

Early British settlers couldn't identify the strange ungainly creature. They assumed it was a relative of the more familiar guinea fowl, an African species that had long been hunted for food. In those days guinea fowl weren't bred in captivity, they were wild caught, then imported live and carried around the Eastern Mediterranean, often passing through Constantinople. Because of their point of entry into Europe, everyone knew them as turkey-fowl, and this name was transferred to the giant American birds that were no relation. Today the scientific name for the wild turkey is *meleagris gallopavo*, meleagris being Greek for guinea fowl.

The first record we have of live turkeys appearing on this side of the Atlantic is 1519 in Spain. They didn't arrive in Britain until around 1526, courtesy of a wealthy Yorkshireman by the name of William Strickland. In his young days Strickland wandered the New World with Italian explorer Sebastian Cabot and from one such voyage brought back with him six of these huge unfamiliar birds. Strickland sold the first turkeys very cheaply as few people were convinced that the strange looking creatures could be edible. When it was realised that turkey meat was tasty, demand and price both shot up. More were imported and were breathtakingly expensive. Some buyers thought they were too costly to simply eat, and kept the turkeys for their novel aesthetic value. Strickland made a considerable amount of money from importing turkeys and later adopted the bird as an emblem on his personal coat of arms; this is the earliest known representation of a turkey in Europe.

At first the birds were all imported live but farmers quickly learned how to successfully breed the new arrivals. Local production brought down the price and turkey meat became increasingly popular but still only amongst the affluent. For a long time it remained a luxury food that was beyond the reach of most pockets.

Henry VIII was the first monarch to have turkey for Christmas, but that's hardly surprising as he was always eager to experiment with new foods. Towards the end of his reign Henry was particularly fond of Christmas Pie. This was a monumental meal consisting of a coffin shaped pie crust containing a turkey that was stuffed with a goose which was stuffed with a chicken which was stuffed with a partridge which was stuffed with a pigeon. Just to ensure that no-one left the table hungry there were side orders of hare, game birds, ducks and geese. It's no surprise that Henry went from a slim athletic young man into bloated middle age.

The Wishbone

Wishbones have been the subject of superstition since ancient times. Making a wish on a wishbone dates back over 2000 years to the Etruscans in Italy. It was believed that chickens were soothsayers who

Roast turkey has become the centrepiece of Christmas lunch, even though there is nothing particularly seasonal about the bird.

could predict the future using grains of corn in a manner similar to an Ouija board. When one of these 'hen oracles' was killed, the collarbone was dried and later stroked to make a wish. Scarcity of the sacred birds and collarbones heralded the practice of breaking them in order to have more wishes to go around.

Today, pulling the dried *furcula* or V-shaped collarbone and snapping the bone in two takes place between the little fingers of two "wishers". The wish of the person getting "the lucky break" (holding the longer piece of bone) is predicted to come true. The loser gets "a bad break" – or loses the chance of making a wish. The winner of this contest may choose to give the fragment of wishbone, along with the wish, to a person of his or her choosing.

Long before the turkey tradition, the goose-bone was used in Medieval Europe. In the 15th Century it was believed that the wishbone could be used to predict the weather. Geese were thought to be oracle birds through which a deity might speak about the future. In 1455, Dr. Hartlieb, a Bavarian physician, wrote: "When the goose has been eaten on St. Martin's Day or Night, the oldest and most sagacious keeps the breast-bone and allowing it to dry until the morning examines it all around, in front, behind and in the middle. Thereby they divine whether the winter will be severe or mild, dry or wet, and are so confident in their prediction that they will wager their goods and chattels on its accuracy."

Stuffing

Stuffing is now one of the key trimmings for a Christmas turkey, it's part of the flavours that make up the meal but this wasn't always the case. Historians think it was first used for a much more practical reason. Humans have known for thousands of years that meat must be prepared before eating. Animals need to be carefully dressed, as cooking the intestines would ruin the feast. Grand houses always roasted

Sage and onion stuffing was tasty, inexpensive and promoted good health.

poultry on a rotating spit above a fire but that's impossible when the internal organs have been removed and the bird is hollow. Early stuffing was used to pack the bird tight so it stayed firm on the spit and could be turned. Obviously the stuffing had to be edible and people experimented with different recipes. It was eventually noticed that the choice of packing affected the taste of the meat. Cooks tried different combinations and over time modern stuffing was invented.

In the 19th Century it was very fashionable for doctors to dismiss folk remedies as 'old wives' tales', now we've learned that very often those old wives knew what they were doing. Cures and treatments become popular over the years because they were effective, they've evolved through many generations, tried and tested by people with a real knowledge of plant use. Today these traditional treatments form the basis of many hi-tech medicines. And so it was with stuffing.

The ingredients of stuffing are varied – breadcrumbs, sausage meat, chestnuts and fruit are all popular today. But it's no coincidence that, historically, the most frequently used recipes were based on sage and onion, two of the most effective and accessible foods that could be used to reduce the risk of food poisoning. Through years of trial and error it was realised that this combination not only saved lives but also a great deal of discomfort. Cooks experimented and noted what caused problems and what solved them - proving how skilful as proto-chemists they were.

Sage had been used to prepare meat, enhance taste and protect from harmful bugs for centuries. Its scientific name is *salvia*, from the Latin word *salvare* meaning 'to cure'. The herb's leaves contain a volatile oil called *thujone* which is a powerful natural antiseptic. Sage was widely used as a mouthwash and, infused in water, to clean wounds.

In the Middle Ages onions were added to the mix. These extraordinary vegetables, like sage, contain natural antiseptics but also have antibacterial properties. Recent research proves beyond doubt that the chemicals in onions are extremely good at limiting the growth of *Campylobacter*, the bacteria largely responsible for food poisoning, something frequently found in poultry that has not been stored properly or is undercooked. Both were everyday problems in pre-refrigerator Tudor England.

The accumulated wisdom of the kitchen was passed on through families and the end result became part of a modern, healthier, Christmas.

Television and the Delia Effect: How Cranberries became stars.

Although we associate the cranberry with North America, this tiny fruit is found over most of the Northern Hemisphere, including Europe and Asia. They come from evergreen shrubs, related to bilberries and blueberries, found in acidic bogs in cool, temperate zones. Humans have been harvesting and eating cranberries for millennia. They were introduced to early European settlers by Algonquin Indians in Massachusetts, the place where we first encountered turkeys. The Algonquins knew the fruit as *sassamanash* and used it for food, dye and wound dressings. The settlers soon came up with their own name, they thought that the shape of the flowers resembled the head of a crane and called it the craneberry; quickly shortened to the form we use now. The cranberry crop is usually abundant and concentrated, the fruit needs to be collected quickly. In the 17th Century humans had competition as wild bears moved in for their share of the bonanza. Both species would hold their ground to reap the harvest and there were regular casualties on both sides.

Cranberries become ripe in late autumn and, as the Thanksgiving Day holiday always falls on the 4th Sunday of November, they were inevitably incorporated, as sauce, into the Thanksgiving Dinner. This is one of the festive highlights of the North American calendar and, traditionally, featured roast turkey – hence the two quickly became table-companions.

Commercial cranberry farming started in Cape Cod, Canada in 1816 but the fruit didn't make an impression in Britain until the 1970s and even then it was not enormously popular. The turning point came in 1995 when TV chef Delia Smith featured fresh cranberries in her cookery series on winter foods: *The Winter*

Cranberries are rich in proanthocyanidins, chemicals believed to reduce the risk of coronary heart disease and protect the urinary tract wall. The berries are harvested in autumn by flooding the cranberry patches and the ripe berries float off to be collected by machine.

Collection. Britain went cranberry crazy, the day after broadcast sales rose by 200 per cent and there was an immediate nationwide shortage. The term 'Delia effect' entered the Collins English Dictionary in 2001 – it refers to impact that a recommendation from Delia has on the purchasing public – cranberries being the original example. Since 1996 we have imported a huge quantity of seasonal berries from America and Canada, and home-made cranberry sauce has become an established Christmas indulgence.

Until very recently the introduction of new Christmas treats has been the result of travellers pushing geographical boundaries and returning with unfamiliar foods that seize the imagination. Today, as Delia illustrates, that role has been taken over in part by television. In the future new festive dishes and ingredients may reach our tables through sophisticated and beautifully produced programming.

Arguably, television plays another unexpected role in these ancient rituals. As the sale of artificial trees slowly increases, we're abandoning the tradition of bringing living greenery into the house in mid winter. Meanwhile other, newer 'traditions' are being formed, including the scheduling of more natural history programmes on television during the Christmas holidays, particularly on New Year's Day. In these gloomy, wet and cold days we can watch animals and plants in seasonal snow or alluring sunshine reminding us of brighter times and of our place within other orders of living things. We experience a sense of connectedness through these glimpses of the natural world. This is surely the modern hi-tech echo of bringing evergreens indoors bearing the promise of better times to come.

The Ghost of Lunches Past

For almost the whole of the first millennium following the birth of Jesus, Christmas was just one holy day amongst many. It certainly wasn't the popular cultural event

William the Conqueror and his men landed at Pevensey, Sussex on September 28th 1066 and helped established Christmas on the British calendar.

we recognise today. If at all, most people would have marked it by going to church, there certainly wouldn't have been either the time or resources to prepare special food. The day's importance slowly increased for more secular reasons. Several influential kings, Charlemagne in 800AD, Edward the Martyr in 855 and William the Conqueror in 1066, all chose to be crowned on Christmas Day to underline the fact that they had been selected to rule by divine power. These decisions meant that by the 13th Century Christmas had developed into a major feast.

The first recorded British Christmas lunch menu dates back to the coronation of William the Conqueror in Westminster Abbey – in 1066. The name Norman is a shortened form of Norseman, William and his men were the direct descendants of Viking invaders that raided and settled

The wild boar hunt was a dangerous activity that frequently ended in failure. These animals can run at 50 kms per hour when chased and are a serious adversary for the hunter. They were once common in Britain but disappeared around the 15th Century. However they have now re-established themselves and wild boar breed in many parts of the country, descendants of escapees from private collections.

in north-west France two hundred years earlier. In addition to swords, axes and extraordinary boats, all very useful when it came to the invasion, the Norsemen carried with them traditions that originated in Scandinavia which transferred to France and then onto England.

One of the most powerful of the Nordic deities was Freya (from whom Friday takes its name) who was strongly associated with the winter solstice. To honour Freya a roast wild boar was eaten on mid-winter's day, a tradition William's men took with them to Hastings. As new rulers their rituals took precedence and were incorporated into the celebrations. The focal-point of the dinner on Christmas Day, following William's coronation, was wild boar.

The choice of wild boar wasn't accidental, Freya was thought to travel across the skies in a chariot pulled by a golden boar, Hildisvíni. She was associated with many other animals (such as cats and falcons) yet their symbolism was ignored in the festivities. The boar claimed the focus because it was perceived to be the strongest and most dangerous of all prey animals. A big male boar is powerful, fearless and armed with massive tusks, he is perfectly capable of killing a human. Only the bravest and most skilled huntsmen could

Hunting boar was a high status activity for Norman landowners.

bring down a fully grown wild boar. Eating these animals wasn't just about food, it was designed to display dominion, strength and authority. Roasting a boar was a way of announcing to the world that here was someone not to be easily challenged. We can see that even in the 11th Century a Public Relations dynamic was well established.

It was December 25th 1066 and the most notable people in the land were present at the coronation of William. When it was seen that the invited nobility had boar for Christmas lunch, it set a trend amongst the elite which, over decades, gradually moved country-wide. However, because eating boar was such a potent symbol of power, rich

Serving the boar's head at Christmas was usually accompanied by music and singing. There is even a 16th century carol that celebrates the dish: The Boar's Head Carol.

landowners colluded to make it difficult for the less wealthy to indulge. Few had real hope of doing so as it was only affluent hunters that had weapons good enough to bring down such formidable animals. Nonetheless, records show that the inventive, and hungry, peasants came up with a variety of ways to hunt boar using pit traps and dogs. However it was a risky business. In those days boar lived wild throughout the country but most of the best hunting areas were in woodlands owned by the aristocracy and protected by a draconian piece of legislation known as the Forest Law. Anyone found poaching could be hung, castrated, blinded, have hands severed or suffer almost any other bloodthirsty punishment conjured by the landowner. Understandably this did a reasonable job of ensuring that few people had wild boar for Christmas!

Interestingly, those aspiring and more affluent households that couldn't afford a real boar's head attempted to boost their status by crafting one from pastry. These heads were heavily salted before cooking and were completely inedible underlining that the boar's head was a social statement not a foodstuff.

This elitism meant that for centuries roast boar remained the nobility's festive meal of choice, the highlight being the presentation

People lacking the resources to hunt a real boar for Christmas would often create a symbolic one from heavily salted dough. When baked hard this was inedible but implied affluence and plenty at the dining table.

of the head. It was carried in ceremoniously and the richest of families placed an orange in the boar's mouth to represent the returning sun. But for many noble houses oranges were too expensive a symbol and so they served the boar with an apple in its mouth. Food historians believe that this practice is the origin of today's tradition of eating ham at Christmas. The cold ham dressed with apple sauce often consumed over the festive period may unknowingly recreate another solstice ritual that dates back to the Vikings.

So, to illustrate just one of the multicultural underpinnings of the Christmas festival, a French nobleman was crowned King of England using a Scandinavian pagan ritual to acknowledge a Christian festival on a date fixed by the Romans recalling an event that took place in Judea one thousand years earlier. Could there be a better illustration of the cultural and geographical diversity that makes Christmas unique?

FUR AND FEATHERS FLYING
Peacock

One of the more unlikely historical Christmas dishes was roast peacock. The word peacock refers to the male of a species technically called peafowl, originally from the forests of the Indian subcontinent. The males' spectacular tails made these birds very

Roast Peacock was designed to be a visual feast rather than an edible one. Although the display required a substantial table as fully grown peacocks can weigh 6 kgs, with a tail that is 2 metres across.

popular ornamental additions to the gardens of great houses for thousands of years. Peacocks were highly valued in Greek and Kurdish art and are the National Bird of India. Their distinctive 'eye feathers' appear in cultures around the world. Viking warriors were buried with them and European medieval knights wore them in their helmets before going into battle.

Peacocks first arrived in Britain with the Romans, who seldom went anywhere without them. They were kept in pens and closely guarded as they were extremely valuable. These ostentatious birds were definitely not for the garden, they were destined for the table. Records confirm that they were eaten for exactly the same reasons of display, which is just as well because contemporary reports tell us that peacock meat was unpleasant and far too tough to enjoy. *Apicius* is a Roman cookbook written in the 4th Century AD, it describes peacock meat as being suitable only for rissoles. But that rather missed the point, serving peacock was an index to wealth and acted more as a table decoration than as a food – it was conspicuous consumption writ large.

Few peacocks survived once the Romans left, they probably fell prey to the wolves and other predators that still thrived in Britain. Almost certainly they weren't eaten

A 16th centur[y] feast serving roast and decorated peacock.

by the locals as Anglo-Saxon texts advised people against peacock meat as it was too stringy to be easily digested. The bird then disappears from English literature until the 13th Century, when it emerges as a Christmas lunch. By then roast boar was passé and the nobility needed new exotic dishes to display and they chose male peafowl. It was, however, essential that the bird was served correctly. Unlike poultry, before going onto the spit peacocks weren't plucked but completely skinned, this was a skilful task that required the skin and feathers to be removed in one piece to use in display later. One contemporary recipe instructs the cook "when he is roasted enough, take him off, and let him cool; and then wind the skin with the feathers and the tail about the body, and serve him forth as if he was alive". The idea was to have a

Britain has three species of swan. Bewick and whooper swans are winter visitors from the north and very difficult to catch. It was the widespread and approachable mute swans that featured on dining tables. Although called mute, these birds produce a wide range of sounds from hissing and snorting to barking and croaking. And, contrary to the widespread belief, a blow from a swan's wing is not sufficiently strong to break a human leg.

living peacock, complete with tail in full display, sitting in the centre of the table. It may have looked dramatic, but the presentation didn't improve the taste and peacocks were finally abandoned as a main course by the 17th Century.

Swan

For the aristocracy, flamboyance was the key to the year's most important feast and there was one native bird that fitted the bill perfectly – the mute swan. Because of their size and presence swans were seen as such a powerful symbol that laws were passed in the 12th Century granting possession of all swans on the River Thames and in open water to the Monarchy, ensuring that only royal favourites could dine on this regal dish. To this day, the Monarch of the United Kingdom retains the right to all mute swans in open water, but only exercises ownership on certain stretches of the River Thames and its surrounding tributaries. Though, it must be said, swans are no longer eaten.

700 years ago a small number of culled swans annually made their way onto the open market, raising money for the crown. For nearly three centuries it was the most expensive meat in the country, even though it was thought to have a thoroughly unpleasant

Festivities in the Middle Ag involved eatin a huge variety of wild anima hedgehogs, herons, seals, cormorants ar gulls have all been recorded ancient menu

taste. However the primary aim wasn't to eat the swan but to be *seen* eating the swan. There are reliable reports of aspiring households inviting an audience to watch them feasting on this high-status bird for Christmas. This is what sociologists call invidious consumption, where people overtly indulge in expensive goods as a way of provoking envy and displaying superior rank.

Adult swans were so tough and unpalatable that the finest hosts often served only cygnets for Christmas. The trouble with cygnets is that they are grey, lacking the pure white plumage of adults. Canny cooks would often use two birds for important meals. They cooked a cygnet but then served it inside the skin of an adult swan. So the meat would be tender but the presentation would still look impressive. Swans were kept by most land-owners and full-time herders were paid to protect the birds against poachers and predators. Swans were on the menu for more than 500 years.

As recently as 1840 Queen Victoria and her family last sat down in Windsor Castle to dine on roast swan for Christmas lunch. There were also side dishes of turbot, rabbit, turkey, larks, pheasants, partridge and the inevitable boar's head.

Red Squirrel

For about 400 years one of the most sought after side-orders at Christmas lunch was red squirrel cooked in butter and parsley. Unlike most animals, squirrels have a hard time finding food in summer but thrive in late autumn when the nut harvest appears. By winter they are fat, healthy and were once very popular on the tables of 'great lords'. Red squirrels were then found throughout the country living in woodlands largely governed by Forest Law. By definition any commoner found eating squirrel must have been a poacher and would have faced dire consequences.

Red Squirrels were a common animal in Britain until the 19th Century. They were a popular food at Christmas and, according to records, tasted something like chicken. Grey squirrels weren't a dining option as they weren't introduced from America until approximately 1876.

49

Wild greylag geese are wary and extremely difficult to approach. They usually feed in groups and keep a sharp eye open for danger. It is almost impossible to get closer than 100 meters to these birds, before they take to the air. Hence the expression 'wild goose chase'.

Goose
Christmas is coming, the goose is getting fat...

Farmyard geese are the direct descendants of the greylag goose, a species that still lives in northern Europe. Wild greylags are creatures of windswept landscapes, they are found in marshes and remote lakes, well away from humans. They are one of the most wary and timid of all birds but if young geese are collected from nests as soon as they hatch, they will imprint on their captors and become tame. Humans first domesticated geese at least 5000 years ago and quickly learned to breed them. To build their stock, hunters just had to go out into the wilds in spring and collect more eggs that were close to the point of hatching. The growing flocks provided meat, feathers, eggs, fat and an excellent alarm system. Geese are highly territorial and create a ruckus when someone unfamiliar approaches.

Nutritionally geese may be tasty and full of calories but they are slow to rear. A newly hatched gosling takes more than 6 months to reach maturity and, even then, only provides just one meal for a family. Most people kept geese for their eggs, a resource that produced food regularly for many months, rather than for their meat. The bird would normally only be eaten once her laying days were over. A goose bred exclusively for eating was an expensive luxury and kept for just one special occasion.

Country folk usually had access to at least one goose a year, they could kill one of their own aging egg-layers or barter one from a neighbour. They might even have access to a wild population nearby. But these options weren't available to everyone. Human history shows a slow but relentless movement of people migrating from the countryside into towns. City life may have had its advantages but goose-rearing was certainly not one of them. Geese need space and water, they are grazing waterfowl that

Geese are birds of open spaces, they do not thrive when kept in cramped conditions.

Goose selling was a famously chaotic event, bringing together buyers and hundreds of geese that had never before been handled. Buyers knew where the sale was taking place because of the noise.

require constant access to rich meadows and unpolluted ponds. Geese will die if kept in cramped conditions. This problem simply offered a new business opportunity to the savvy entrepreneurs of Middle Age Britain. Geese were in high demand by city-dwellers at Christmas but they couldn't provide their own, while people in rural areas had plenty of geese that no local needed to buy.

Farmers solved this conundrum by breeding the birds in the country and transporting them for sale in the cities. Logistically this journey was a challenge. The geese couldn't be despatched, plucked and dressed before taking them into cities as the meat would spoil. The birds had

to be moved live and that was a slow, laborious task because the creatures had to walk. Herders would take flocks from rural breeding areas and drive them into the cities, the long flight feathers trimmed to prevent them from flying away. Often the birds would have to walk across several counties, there are records of goose gaggles journeying from Devon to London.

However, travelling such distances on dry land is an unnatural act for geese, they are designed to swim or fly. Their short legs and delicately webbed feet are just not suited to cross-country walks. Forced marches presented problems, normally in the wild geese would only walk on soft, springy grass when they were feeding and, even then, they would cover very little distance. If herders drove the geese just half a mile a day along stony roads, their feet would soon become too damaged to walk.

Another concern was loss of body condition and the consequent drop in profit. Geese were sold by weight and the rigours of a rushed marathon would mean that the birds would become very thin as a consequence of the enforced exercise. Hence goose herding had to be an unhurried process, often the flock would take two months to reach market. They needed to walk slowly in order to maintain a good weight and, every day, be allowed time to feed in meadows to stay plump and healthy.

On the day before reaching market goose-herders would buy grain to feed their birds because it is much heaver than grass. The geese would be encouraged to eat as much as possible to increase their weight and selling price. Not until preparing the bird for cooking did unwary buyers discover that they had to throw away a large weight of undigested grain from the bird's stomach. As grain was a lot less expensive than goose, this last minute meal pushed up the herders' profit margin.

Regular pauses to feed kept the birds heavy and valuable but didn't stop the fact that the geese were eroding their feet. There were several available solutions to this dilemma, some people put boots on the geese, made of coarse sacking or leather but they were easily lost. The most widely used and time-honoured protection technique involved walking the geese through hot pitch then immediately over coarse sand. Pitch is made by heating the sap from pine trees. Puddles of warm pitch were built and then geese were driven through so that their feet were completely immersed. While the pitch was still soft, the birds were herded onto loose sand that became embedded into the sticky mess. This mixture then

hardened to a consistency not unlike tarmac, protecting the birds' feet from even the longest walk. Fortunately, geese have very few nerve-endings in their feet.

After a mammoth march the geese would eventually arrive at the urban markets, fit, fat and ready to sell. Roast goose for Christmas dinner was not just a meal it was a mark of success. People would save for months to ensure they could afford a decent bird. Institutions such as pubs set up 'goose clubs' (a forerunner of today's Christmas Clubs) allowing savers to put away a few pennies a week in preparation for the first goose-fair. But buying a bird was just the start of the festive problems as it then had to be cooked.

The feet of geese are perfect for swimming, but cannot withstand the rigours of month-long marches.

There was just one way to serve a Christmas goose and that was to roast it, but very few people had ovens, even wall-mounted fireplaces were rare in most houses until the end of the 17th Century. On the rare occasions when meat was roasted it almost always took place outdoors, this caused no difficulties in rural areas, there was fuel in the form of timber and always somewhere safe to build a fire. It was very different in cities. Few people had gardens and, even those that did, were almost always surrounded by houses made entirely of wood. Building an open fire in a 15th Century British city was terribly dangerous and would not have been greeted kindly by neighbours.

For centuries most people ate food that was cooked in a metal pot above a fire.

For centuries most cooking was done on an open fire, with every ingredient of the meal simmering in just one pot.

Only the wealthy had separate ovens or fires large enough for spit-roasts. When aspiring gourmets wanted roast goose they had to hire an oven. From the middle of December it often became quite difficult to find bread in built-up areas, as bakers realised that they had an important resource at their disposal, at least for the next two weeks. Many temporarily abandoned their normal fare, suspended the bread business and rented out the ovens for goose roasting.

Understandably everyone wanted their roast ready for Christmas day but there were many more geese than ovens, so the wily bakers raised the oven-rent charges on the morning of Christmas Eve. Less affluent townsfolk were already stretching their finances to buy the bird, so they often had to opt for a less expensive cooking session and that was always a few days before the 25th. This is a risky strategy, in a time before fridges poultry meat was a major source of food poisoning. It's impossible to know the statistics but public health experts believe there must have been thousands of cases every year brought about by this staggered cooking system.

Commoners – away from the grand houses

History tends only to record the everyday lives of the wealthy; details of other lives go unnoticed. It's important to remember that until recently Christmas Day for the poor was like any other, employees weren't given a day off and celebrations were confined to an extra Mass at the local church. As recently as Victorian times most workers, if they were lucky, would receive only a half-day holiday. This didn't leave much time for the preparation of special foods, even if the resources were available. For most people providing enough food of any kind in winter was a challenge, treats were out of the question and Christmas day as a full holiday is a recent phenomenon.

Bakers in the Middle Ages ceased producing bread at Christmas, in favour of something much more lucrative.

Historians believe that Christmas lunch for most people during the largest part of the last 2000 years would have been exactly the same as any other day. There are a few suggestions that rabbits and hares might occasionally have been on the menu. But even that meat would probably have been scarce, fish is much more likely. Because it was seen as a less valuable resource than red meat, poaching fish posed less of a risk than poaching on land.

Italian Takeaway

The Roman army reached British shores in 43AD and remained for 350 years; their time here was, gastronomically, the most important in our history. The invaders were unimpressed with our native cuisine and, once settled, soon imported familiar foods that they found more palatable. Many of these were new to Britain and went on to become integral to Christmas. Emperor Claudius' men gave us onions, mint, thyme, garlic, shallots, rosemary, sage, sweet chestnuts, cabbage, beet, lettuce, apples, peas and wine. Our celebrations would be flavoured very differently without the Roman influence.

Roast Chestnuts

The only native chestnut in Britain is the conker or horse chestnut, *Aesculus hippocastanum*. The myth that its glossy brown seeds are deadly is an exaggeration, they are however toxic and eating just one will cause severe nausea and stomach cramps. The chestnuts we prize at Christmas – sweet chestnuts known also as the Spanish or European Chestnut - come from a different species of tree, *Castanea sativaonce*, originally found only in Southern Europe, western Asia and north Africa. Brought here by the Romans, it is now regarded as an 'honorary native' – and is found throughout Britain especially in southern England.

Sweet chestnuts were an important food source in Southern Europe for centuries. They can be roasted, made into flour, pureed and, in Corsica, are used to make beer.

Pottage was a popular meal in the Middle Ages. It is served here in the Peasant Wedding by Peter Breugel the Elder, painted in 1567.

Favoured as landscaping trees during the 18th & 19th centuries, sweet chestnuts have also been planted extensively in parkland, where some of our most ancient examples can be located. Sadly, our climate is not ideal for sweet chestnut production - the nuts produced by trees in Italy, Spain and France, tend to be larger than those produced in Britain. Many nuts fail to develop fully in our temperate, cooler climate. Historically, sweet chestnuts grown here were often fed to pigs for this reason.

Christmas Pudding

Although traditional domed Christmas puddings are highly visible when British festivities are shown in films, paintings and illustrations, less than 50% of the population now eat them after lunch. Puddings have been overtaken by ice-cream as the desert of choice. However, many people still retain the childhood memory of a flaming pudding being ceremoniously carried to the Christmas table. But the contemporary creation is a great departure from the original.

Puddings arrived in England with the Normans, but then the word referred specifically to blood sausage, a type of black pudding, and it was strictly a savoury dish. Traditionally, many pigs were slaughtered in late autumn, after they'd fattened up on acorns and fallen fruit. It was uneconomic to retain every animal throughout winter as they would eat much and provide little in return. Farmers culled their herds keeping most of their females and a small number of best quality males, ready to breed a new herd in the spring. Surplus males and older pigs were dispensable and could be used to provide valuable meat in winter.

It's said that cooks used every piece of the culled pig apart from the 'oink'. Even blood wasn't wasted; it was mixed with cereals, onions and whatever herbs were available and stuffed into washed sections of the pigs' intestines to produce sausage. Because of the timing of the slaughter, black pudding was popular at Christmas. Although pigs

The arrival of the pudding was one of the highlights of a Victorian Christmas. Puddings were round because they had been made in a cloth bag and boiled for many hours.

were the main source of puddings, any farm-stock could be used. One unlikely 15th Century recipe tells us how to prepare porpoise pudding – a sausage made from porpoise blood. These animals were never easy to catch, so porpoise pudding was exclusive to the aristocracy.

British blood puddings often contained oatmeal and barley as fillers. When exotic spices appeared in Britain, they were added to the mixture and, as with most recipes, the flavour constantly evolved. This method of cooking allowed lots of ingredients to be blended together and infused into a whole. It was practical, economical and adapted into many forms, including the haggis. Soon the word 'pudding' was used to describe any savoury food created using a process similar to sausage-making where meat and other ingredients in a semi-liquid form were encased and then steamed or boiled to set the contents.

At around the same time a staple part of the British diet was a grim sounding dish called plum pottage. This was a meat soup, thickened with breadcrumbs and livened up a little with a handful of plums. It was made at the tail end of the year and people added whatever was at hand. The few reports we have tell us that plum pottage tasted like a very thick, fruity stew. Some recipes called for the addition of wheat and sugar and, at some stage, a smart cook decided to try a new cooking method. Inventive Elizabethans decided to wrap a thin cotton cloth tightly around the uncooked mixture and then boil the whole thing to produce a solid mass that could be sliced. At this stage dark sugar or molasses still hadn't arrived in Britain, so the first recognisable incarnations of Christmas pudding would have seemed very pale and anaemic to our eyes. The resulting dish could contain a huge range of ingredients but, above all, it was sweet.

Today Christmas puddings are still one of the richest and calorie-laden dishes of the year.

It was the sweetness that most people craved and eventually meat was dropped from the recipe. Over the years other exotic additions were slipped into the blend, including brandy and claret. At its best this dish had evolved into just about the richest single item of food eaten by ordinary people and it absorbed a great many costly resources.

By the 17th Century Christmas puddings were unbridled hedonism on a plate, some authorities believed that they were just too dangerous to be allowed out amongst the general population! After the English

Oliver Cromwell was not solely responsible for banning Christmas celebrations. The decision was taken by the entire Parliament. But it's Old Ironsides who has gone down in history as the first Scrooge.

Civil War, the monarchy was temporarily overthrown following the execution of Charles 1 and the country became a republic overseen by the puritanical Oliver Cromwell. He wasn't keen on any kind of unrestrained celebration, whatever the focus. In 1647 the ruling Parliamentary Party passed an Ordinance abolishing the feasts of Christmas, Easter and Whitsun, shops and businesses were ordered to remain open on December 25th. Fines were imposed on anyone found celebrating the festival. Although against the law, Christmas was still observed by many people but quietly and behind closed doors. Not only was it illegal to celebrate the day, it was also against the law to partake in any of the traditional foods associated with it. Meat was exempt from the ban as it was a normal part of everyday life, but celebratory cakes and puddings were completely forbidden. Christmas pudding was struck from the menu.

Execute a monarch and most of the population will tut, frown and then carry on with life, after all few of his subjects had ever seen King Charles. But take away a British person's pud and there'll be blood on the streets. In London there were violent clashes between Government enforcers and supporters of Christmas and all its excesses. Canterbury witnessed the famous Plum Pudding Riots in 1658. To quell them Cromwell sent 3,000 armed men to break down the city gates and enforce the ban. Many hundreds of the protesters were injured trying to defend their dessert.

In 1664 Oliver Cromwell called the dish "a lewd custom …unfit for God-fearing people". There was to be no easy reprieve for the Christmas pudding until Charles II returned and, even then, it made a slow comeback as the taste and recipe had slipped from public consciousness. Then along came genial King George I, a tolerant monarch with a sweet tooth. He tried a Christmas pudding in 1714 and declared it to be

THE EMPIRE CHRISTMAS PUDDING

according to the recipe supplied by the King's Chef Mr. CEDARD, with Their Majesties' Gracious Consent

1 lb	Currants	Australia
1 lb	Sultanas	Australia or South Africa
1 lb	Stoned Raisins	Australia or South Africa
5 ozs	Minced Apple	United Kingdom or Canada
1 lb	Bread Crumbs	United Kingdom
1 lb	Beef Suet	United Kingdom
6½ ozs	Cut Candied Peel	South Africa
8 ozs	Flour	United Kingdom
8 ozs	Demerara Sugar	British West Indies or British Guiana
5	Eggs	United Kingdom or Irish Free State
½ oz	Ground Cinnamon	India or Ceylon
¼ oz	Ground Cloves	Zanzibar
¼ oz	Ground Nutmegs	British West Indies
¼ teaspoon	Pudding Spice	India or British West Indies
¼ gill	Brandy	Australia · S. Africa Cyprus or Palestine
¼ gill	Rum	Jamaica or British Guiana
1 pint	Beer	England · Wales · Scotland or Ireland

WRITE TO THE EMPIRE MARKETING BOARD, WESTMINSTER, FOR A FREE BOOKLET ON EMPIRE CHRISTMAS FARE GIVING THIS AND OTHER RECIPES.

In the 1920s the Empire Marketing Board came up with the idea of promoting Christmas pudding recipes that included ingredients from all corners of the British Empire.

delicious. However, his enthusiasm wasn't universally shared, and there was still a strong echo of Cromwell's violent opposition. After it became known that the King had resurrected this tempting morsel, London's Quakers described the pudding as "the invention of the scarlet whore of Babylon." Of course any dish on the receiving end of such colourfully bad publicity will immediately become enormously popular. Christmas puddings became virtually obligatory.

Mince Pies

These ubiquitous Christmas delicacies have had a long and tortuous journey to reach the form that we know today. The first written reference dates back to 1557, but at that time they were called shred pies. When an animal was slaughtered the best joints were simply carved while the less valued meat was often cunningly disguised before being brought to table. At Christmas the innards, or umbles, of wild boar were put into a pastry crust and baked to produce Umble Pie. But that often left a pile of miscellaneous bits or 'shreds'. These were minced and added to chopped suet, hard animal fat that

Individual mince pies were designed to be eaten while travelling.

no-one liked to eat, and used to make lower grade pies that required extra ingredients to make them palatable. This is how they earned their later name of minced pies. Elizabethans added cloves, mace, pepper, raisins and prunes to disguise the flavour of what would, otherwise, have been a less-than-tasty dish. Even with the addition of dried fruit, this was still a savoury meal rather than a dessert. Early shred pies were cooked in huge slabs that were sliced and shared by everyone.

Eventually it was discovered that if the fruit was soaked in brandy or other alcohol before cooking then the taste would improve, and by all accounts the pie desperately needed improving! Good cooks plan ahead and soon, in autumn, when apples and plums were harvested they were immediately stored in alcohol in jars, ready to put into pies in winter. Shreds of meat would be added to the pies at the last moment, but eventually the meat was omitted as it spoiled the flavour. Soon cookbooks featured recipes for 'minced pies without meat'.

Cromwell, in Puritanical fervour, not only banned Christmas puddings but also specifically outlawed mince pies as they too were considered to be sinful. Eating, selling or cooking them could again result in heavy fines. The pies disappeared from the open market and didn't re-emerge until Charles II was crowned. After years of Puritanical restrictions, England breathed a sigh of relief and effectively had one huge party. They ate and drank too much, anything that had been specifically prohibited by Cromwell was celebrated with glee. By then more spices and sugar were being imported and prices were dropping. A fine, rich mince pie was high on everyone's Christmas list. Now, instead of being a working class confection, they became popular with the whole country. Mince pies were often given to departing guests, providing something tasty to eat while journeying home, because of this many 18th Century cookery books called them 'wayfaring pies'. To make them easier to carry, the pies became discrete, small enough to eat with one hand while travelling. Instead of being a small chunk of a larger whole, each pie had its own sealed pastry case, just as it does today.

Incidentally Cromwell's law banning mince pies has never been overturned so, technically, they remain illegal. The British eat, on average, 28 mince pies per person at Christmas. That's more than one billion pies, a truly impressive nationwide crime wave!

Although there is no logical reason for mince pies to be eaten only at Christmas, our traditions are so powerful that few people would buy, make or eat them at any other time of the year.

Victorian Mince Pie – with real meat
From the 1851 cookbook
Modern Domestic Cookery by A. Lady
(Maria Rundell)

Makes 10 meal size pies
Mince meat:
450g sirloin steak, finely chopped
450g grated suet
4 large apples, peeled, cored and chopped
1.35kg currants
½ small loaf day-old bread, grated
Freshly grated nutmeg, to taste
Ground cinnamon, to taste
Ground cloves, to taste
Ground ginger, to taste
Salt and freshly ground black pepper
450g sugar
2 lemons, zest and juice
Juice of 3 large oranges
Candied peel, diced (optional)
250ml brandy
250ml ruby port
Short crust pastry:
225g flour, plus extra for dusting
115g butter or margarine,
Water, as necessary
4-6 tsp milk
1 tsp sugar

TUDOR LEGACIES

By a quirk of history many of the mainstays of today's traditional Christmas dinner arrived around the same time in the 16th Century. This is no co-incidence as it was during the reigns of Henry VIII and Elizabeth I that Britain's ships sailed out to explore the globe and bring back anything of value or interest. Some discoveries made a grand impact.

Potatoes

The ubiquitous potato originated in South America, somewhere in the Peruvian Andes. First cultivated and harvested around 7000 years ago, they were a vitally important food source to the Incas but were unknown elsewhere. It was not until the Spanish conquistadors arrived that these and other South American plants, such as maize and tomatoes, reached the outside world. We can't be certain of the exact year of arrival but potatoes appear to have reached Britain around 1590. At first they were treated with great suspicion and were slow to gain popularity, as late as the 1800s there was a noisy group of activists determined to keep the potato out of Britain. However *The Society for the Prevention of an Unwholesome Diet,* a 19th Century opposition group, had little effect and the humble potato was here to stay.

There are around 4000 varieties of potato worldwide and 80 available in Britain. For culinary purposes, varieties are generally differentiated by their waxiness. Floury baking potatoes have more starch than waxy boiling potatoes. The potato you're most likely to find roasted with your Christmas lunch is the King Edward. The King Edward was developed by John Butler of Scotter, Lincolnshire, and launched into the United Kingdom in 1902. It is one of the oldest varieties to still be found in Europe. The Coronation of King Edward VII coincided with the introduction of this cultivar and its name is believed to be a celebration of the event. It is claimed that Butler wrote to Buckingham Palace seeking permission to name his potato after the monarch and that a reply was received granting permission.

The King Edward is renowned for its light fluffy texture, and is ideal for roasting.

Potatoes are now such an integral part of the British diet, it is difficult to imagine our menus before they were introduced.

SPROUTS

Sprouts are a member of the mustard family, a large group of plants found growing wild in Western Europe. Sprouts are related to cabbages, cauliflower and broccoli, together known as the brassicas. An early form of sprouts was cultivated in Italy more than 2000 years ago but the modern strain originated in Belgium, hence the name Brussels Sprout, in the 16th Century. The first written reference to this vegetable dates back to 1587. In mid winter sprouts are an excellent source of vitamin C which is essential for humans and was difficult to obtain for our ancestors in the colder months. Although 400 years ago people knew nothing about the RDA (recommended daily allowance) of vitamins, they had long realised that

Sprouts are rich in fibre and antioxidants, they contain vitamins B6 and K, high levels of vitamin A and nearly three times the amount of vitamin C found in oranges. Nutritionally they were perfect for eating in winter, when other fresh food was scarce.

vegetables were essential to health and well-being. Sprouts are hardy, easy to grow and were quickly adopted by local agriculture. Because of their harvest time sprouts became a seasonal tradition but it's not one that appeals to everyone. In Britain we only eat an estimated 28% of the sprouts we buy, prepare and cook at Christmas. The other 72% are thrown away.

DRIED FRUITS

Until very recently the only naturally sweet foods available to Britons were ripe fruit and honey, this ensured that the taste of sugar was highly prized. Most farms and estates had their own bee hives and professional collectors of wild honey earned a good wage. Honey supplied sweetness in summer but only in relatively small quantities, for the winter fruits were gathered in autumn and then dried slowly indoors. This process of drying reduced their moisture content and concentrated the percentage of sugar. Well-heeled sugar lovers imported dried grapes (sultanas) and apricots while the less affluent made do with homespun apples, pears and plums (prunes).

By Christmas time, when the dried fruits were ready to eat and very sweet, they were added not just to puddings but to savoury dishes. The crop didn't last long into the New Year and there was then a long wait until the following winter to enjoy the rare treat.

SUGAR

While the British were busy trying to gather small amounts of sugar from meagre local resources, on the other side of the world, in New Guinea where it grew wild, the locals had been perfecting the cultivation of sugar cane over 10,000 years. It took many centuries for sugar to migrate from this remote island, but slowly it travelled west and was enthusiastically adopted in India, the Middle East and Africa.

But sugar had little impact in Britain until the events of 1493 were felt. It was during that year that Christopher Columbus took the first sugar cane seedlings to the island of Hispaniola in the Caribbean. The growing conditions were perfect and the crop thrived, producing mountains of sugar and money. By 1550 there were sugar plantations and processing factories in Brazil, Cuba and Jamaica, all producing sugar to send back to the sweet-toothed markets in the Old World. Towards the end of the 16th Century a steady flow of sugar was arriving in Britain. At first it was a very expensive luxury and was treated exactly as a spice,

Sugar cane was once the only plentiful source of added sweetness in our diet. Before its introduction Christmas dining was a much more savoury experience.

it took a while for sugar prices to drop and the commodity to become available to everyone. We immediately added sugar to all our pies whilst still leaving in the original sweeteners of dried fruits. This new trade marked a sea-change in the taste of Christmas. It opened the doors to cakes, trifles, sweets and many of the treats that dominate the festival.

SPICES

Allspice

1493 was a busy year for Columbus, for it was then that he came across the fruits of a wild tree known as *Pimenta dioica* on Jamaica. Locals already used it in their own food and some time later, when it was taken back to Europe and absorbed into our cuisine, we gave it the name of allspice as we believed it combined the flavour of cinnamon, nutmeg, and cloves.

Spices are composed of dried roots, bark, seeds or fruit from plants, used to flavour, colour or preserve food. They are sometimes used to mask unpleasant tastes.

Today spices are inextricably bound to the festive season, even the faintest scent of cinnamon or nutmeg will take us back to Christmases past. But spices aren't seasonal, they contain nothing nutritionally essential in winter and there are no obvious links to the nativity, so it's a surprising connection. The association is more practical than Biblical, scholars believe that aromatic spices were popular at Christmas because they hid the smell of rotting meat. When an animal like a cow or deer was killed for cooking, a huge amount of meat was produced at one time. Even in a large household this would

Today's Christmas flavours have reached us from all around the world. Black pepper originated in India but Vietnam is now the biggest producer. Cloves are the dried flower buds from an Indonesian tree. Nutmeg is the dried seed of a tree found in the Moluccas Islands (once called the Spice Islands). Cinnamon comes from Sri Lanka and bay leaves from laurel trees around the Mediterranean. It was this tree that also provided the laurel wreaths used to symbolise victory in ancient Greece and Rome.

provide food for a whole week. But in the days before refrigeration, the meat would often begin to decay before it was eaten. So spices were rubbed into the flesh to mask the scent and taste of spoilage, meat was too valuable to throw away and had to be consumed however it smelled. The distinctive presence of spices was part of mid-winter food preparation for centuries and, by the time modern technology solved the decomposition problem, they had already become an integral part of Christmas meals.

Cinnamon

One of the most Christmassy of all spices is cinnamon; it almost defines the aroma of the season. Cinnamon can be used in both sweet and savoury dishes. While *Cinnamomum verum* is sometimes considered to be "true cinnamon", most cinnamon on the international market is derived from related species referred to as "*cassia*" to distinguish them from "true cinnamon". The spice itself comes from the inner bark of cinnamon trees that originate in Sri Lanka. It's mentioned in the Bible and in early Greek poetry and has been important for at least 2500 years. Small amounts trickled into Europe during the Middle Ages but it didn't become widely accessible to the west until the 16th Century when Portuguese traders opened up a post in Sri Lanka (then still known as Ceylon) and shipped the dried bark back to eager buyers. A packing plant was built; it handled so much cinnamon that the spice could be smelt far out to sea. Sailors reported that it was the 'sweetest port' in the world.

Cinnamon trees are coppiced to encourage them to produce plenty of shoots from ground level. The tree needs to be three years old before harvesting can begin, the delicate and skilled process hasn't changed for thousands of years. Every six months the green shoots are cut and kept under sacking in peeling sheds, this starts the drying process. Then 'peelers' move in to carefully remove and discard the outer bark, this is a delicate operation as it is easy to cut too deeply and take off the soft inner tissue that produces the spice itself. Once the bark is free the raw cinnamon, still on the shoots, is beaten with special hammers to soften the material and lift it from the wood. With a small curved knife, called a *kokaththa*, the cinnamon is separated from the twig, experienced peelers do this in whole sheets. Shredded cinnamon fetches a lower price than intact rolls. Once again the cinnamon is left to dry and this time it curls and takes on the shape of the original twig, producing the characteristic rolls (or quills) of the cinnamon we buy today.

Cinnamon's association with Christmas, again, comes from the fact that it was used as a winter meat preservative. Although that particular need has long gone, the scent of this heady spice became so associated with the celebrations that it was hijacked and imported into a long list of other food and drinks. Fewer people now use it with meat, instead cinnamon has become a vital ingredient in biscuits, cakes and puddings.

Oranges

The wild precursors of oranges come from south-east Asia. We know that the tree was cultivated and selectively bred in China at least 3000 years ago. They were a familiar fruit in the Far East but didn't get to Western Europe until the late 15th Century when brought back by Italian and Portuguese traders. Europeans had known about bitter oranges for centuries, they were grown and used for medicinal purposes. However, the arrival of the sweet orange was a sensation and trees were soon planted all around the Mediterranean. For a long time the oranges eaten in Britain were grown in Spain, where the main picking season was late November. Transportation was slow and the fruit didn't reach our shores until around mid-December. In the 21st Century oranges are shipped in from Israel, North Africa and Florida, they are available fresh at any time of the year. Currently people continue to associate them with Christmas but it's likely that this will slowly disappear as new generations can completely ignore the oranges' seasonal availability.

The colour and shape of the orange has long been thought to evoke the sun. This association has been used ceremoniously – in the fruit placed in the roast boar's mouth – and decoratively in the orange pomanders. The pomander is made by studding an orange or other fruit with whole dried cloves and letting it cure dry, after which it may last several years. The pomander perfumes the air, and contents of wardrobes and drawers. By the 17th and 18th century the decorated orange stuck with cloves was frequently mentioned as a Christmas or New Year's custom. In his 1616 Christmas masque, Ben Jonson wrote, "He has an Orange and rosemary, but not a clove to stick in it."

Oranges, to denote wealth and prosperity, frequently feature in the Christmas stockings filled by Santa on Christmas Eve.

Clementines

Named in 1902, a clementine is a variety of mandarin orange (*Citrus reticulata).* The mandarin is a small citrus tree which is said to have gained its name from the bright orange robes worn by the mandarins or public officials of imperial China. Cultivars and crosses between the mandarin and similar citrus fruits include the Satsuma and the Tangerine. They are easy to peel and generally seedless.

Clementines are at the height of their season in winter and they sell in large numbers from mid-November through to January, giving them the nickname "Christmas oranges" in some markets.

Clementines are usually seedless, sweet and are very easy to peel. This made them popular additions to Christmas stockings in the first half of the 20th Century. Just one supplies 60% of the recommended daily intake of vitamin C.

Chutney

Chutneys and pickles are one of the staples of Christmastime feasting, a perfect match for cheese, cold meats, and delicious in turkey sandwiches. How did they come to feature in the celebrations?

One of the perennial problems of winter is the lack of fresh food. Most wild animals can eat only what is available day-by-day, few have the capacity to store for leaner times. Human technology allows us to take advantage of glut harvests; long ago our ancestors learned to preserve food for hungrier periods when it might be needed. 4000 years ago in India cucumbers were stored in highly salted water to stop them rotting, keeping them available for eating at times of the year when none were growing. The salt lowered the pH level of the cucumbers, killing most of the internal bacteria and preventing the rest from multiplying. It's bacteria that cause food to spoil. By 500 BC the technique had become more advanced; vinegar, lemons and spices were added. Instead of being preserved whole, the ingredients were diced to produce a more coherent flavour. But the aim remained the same, to extend the eating season of food that would normally only be available for a short time of the year. Chutney is now often targeted specifically at the Yule market with "Christmas Chutneys" in abundance at the grocers.

The name "chutney" comes from the Sanskrit word *caṭnī*, (pronounced 'chatnee') which means to lick.

21st Century Lunch

Pubs and restaurants all around contemporary Britain start advertising "Traditional English Christmas Lunches" anytime from September onward. But what exactly are they offering ? The meal we know now is relatively new and certainly not British. What happens if we take away the ingredients introduced from distant shores ? Remove turkey and cranberries from America, potatoes from the Andes, peas and herbs from the Mediterranean, sprouts from Belgium and wine (grapes) from Turkey. We would end up with salt and a small pile of bread from the sauce and stuffing.

*On December 26th, or Wren's Day, boys would scour the
countryside looking for wrens to tie to a pole and carry around
while asking for money to fund a village celebration.
Many birds were killed in the process.*

*The lads were known as Wren Boys and the ritual continued
well into the 20th Century. Competing explanations exist for
this custom. Some, taking cue from Celtic mythology, connect
this violence toward wrens with the bird's association with the
old year, making this a Samhain or midwinter sacrifice.*

*The tradition may also have been influenced by later stories
of wrens betraying the Irish soldiers who fought against the
invading Vikings during the 8th-10th Centuries or revealing
the hiding place of Christian martyr Saint Stephen, after
whom the day is named.*

*Nowadays, the ritual consists of "hunting" a fake wren, and
putting it on top of a decorated pole. Then the crowds of
revellers dress up in masks, straw suits and colourful clothing
and parade to music through the towns and villages.*

Christmas Robin

One bird species dominates the Christmas card market: the robin. Sitting on snowy boughs, surrounded by holly berries or wearing Santa hats, images of robins flutter from their envelopes. But why? There are no robins mentioned in the nativity story, and the robin is a year-round garden resident so not specifically associated with winter – even if its plumage does look especially distinct in snow.

The answer to this conundrum is unlikely. Sending cards at Christmas is a relatively new custom, 200 years ago the practice was unknown. Initially a few people began to exchange hand-made cards but the first commercially produced printed card didn't appear until 1843. In the manner of convergent evolution, this coincides with the emergence of a formalised postal system, with advances in printing technology and an increase in literacy amongst the general population.

As card production began to gain momentum publishers wondered what subjects would be most appropriate for the images, early cards look distinctly un-Christmas-like to modern eyes. There were no scenes of quaint thatched cottages in snow, or any hint of the nativity story or Santa Claus and chimneys. Instead manufacturers opted for drawings of fairies and flowers to suggest an approaching springtime theme.

This was a period when relatively few people wrote or received regular letters, and cards made up a significant proportion of the annual post and, lacking firm ideas of quite what to show, manufacturers acknowledged the status of the postmen himself (and all were men in those days) by including pictures of them on their cards! But this didn't mean illustrations of men with delivery sacks – it meant robins! To explain, in 1793 London postmen had been issued with a very distinctive uniform consisting of a black beaver-skin hat, blue waistcoat and, most significantly, a long scarlet coat.

With typical wit, Londoners almost immediately nick-named their unmistakeable red-coated mail carriers, 'robins'. It wasn't postmen who carried letters, but 'robins' who delivered them. A few card manufacturers whimsically mirrored the postmen's slang name in their designs, they commissioned beautifully painted robins (the birds) holding envelopes in their beaks, dropping them through open windows and letter boxes. The idea was picked up by others and robin cards

Robins and holly. Seasonal icons with unlikely association to Yuletide.

soon flocked over the country. The Christmas robin had arrived, courtesy of an 18th Century Royal Mail livery.

Christmas Cards

Commercial greeting cards played an important role in the invention of the modern Christmas. The tradition of sending seasonal messages of good wishes at Christmastime seems to have started in Germany in the 15th Century, but these were individually crafted missives and were more decorated letters than cards. In 1843 Sir Henry Cole, the first Director of London's Victoria and Albert Museum and one of those involved in setting up the Penny Post three years earlier, commissioned John Callcott Horsley to prepare the artwork for a new Christmas venture. He had a batch of cards printed, used some himself and offered the rest for sale, but as they cost the equivalent of an average worker's weekly wage, initial purchases weren't impressive.

But the cards attracted attention and other entrepreneurs experimented by publishing their own versions at lower prices

and within twenty years Christmas cards were part of the seasonal celebrations. This new and lucrative market meant that manufacturers had to explore possible subjects for illustration. Early designs represented the Nativity, Christian symbols, festive objects such as candles and baubles, and other miscellaneous icons of the season such as the snow and wildlife of the northern forests in winter. More imaginative publishers undertook a little research and unearthed old, largely forgotten Christmas traditions and commissioned artists to show them in bright, colourful cards. The paintings featured flaming yule logs, holly wreaths and bunched mistletoe. Historians believe that by the mid 19th Century most people, particularly in cities, had abandoned

The world's first commercially produced Christmas card.

Early commercial Christmas cards showed images that look very unseasonal to our eyes.

The distinctive Victorian postman.

such traditions. But the new Christmas cards acted as a reminder and slowly these habits reappeared, fuelled by a tide of attractive images. Simultaneously, an army of shop-keepers realised that they could now sell seasonal sprigs of holly and mistletoe to their city-based customers which, in the rural areas, had been completely free to collect.

An early Christmas card, establishing a new tradition.

The Dove and the Spirit of Peace

One of the most ancient symbols of peace is the olive branch, which appeared in ancient Greek culture. The dove is the bird of Aphrodite and represents fulfilment in love.

The dove and olive branch are mentioned in the Biblical account of Noah's Ark, they were icons for Jews and early Christians. According to Genesis, a dove was released by Noah after the flood in order to find land; when it returned carrying an olive leaf in its beak, it gave Noah hope of finding land again after the deluge. Noah's dove therefore is a symbol of hopefulness and peace.

In the Gospels a dove is also used to symbolize the Holy Spirit. (In Matthew and Luke the Holy Spirit is compared to a dove at the Baptism of Jesus.) The dove of the Holy Spirit is an attempt to visualise divinity, connoting purity, simplicity, harmony and the soul.

Early Christian art depicted baptism accompanied by a dove carrying an olive branch in its beak and used a similar icon on their burial chambers as a sign of peace. The dove appears in many funerary inscriptions in the Roman catacombs, often accompanied by the words *in pace* (Latin meaning "in peace").

Domestic doves, usually meaning *Columba livia domestica*, were derived from Rock Pigeons, amongst the world's first domesticated birds. Both Mesopotamian cuneiform tablets and Egyptian hieroglyphics mention tame pigeons more than 5,000 years ago.

At Christmastime the dove appears on cards, and as a decoration bringing a promise of peace, hope and joy.

From the very beginning commercial Christmas cards featured animals. In Christian terms, the dove represents the promise of peace brought into the world by the birth of Jesus.

Christmas Tree

Almost every book and newspaper article looking at Christmas traditions tells us that the decorated tree was introduced into Britain by Prince Albert in the 19th Century. In fact, Albert popularised the idea but he didn't pioneer it. In 1800 Queen Charlotte, wife of George III, had a Christmas tree at Buckingham Palace (then known as Buckingham House, it didn't

Queen Victoria and Prince Albert with their Christmas tree in 1848.

become a Royal Palace until 1837), 19 years before Prince Albert was born.

The tradition of bringing trees into houses comes originally from central Europe and dates back centuries. There are many versions of how the custom started. Some say that the tree represents God, others that it is a symbol of future fertility at the darkest, coldest time of the year. We do know that decorated Christmas trees were common in Germany by the end of the 15th Century and the most likely explanation for their appearance in Britain is that they came over with European immigrants. Prince Albert was certainly a fan and appears to have had larger, more lavish trees. Because he lived at a time when the domestic arrangements of the Royal family were less private, Queen Victoria's Christmas preparations at Windsor castle were widely reported, gossiped about and quickly copied. It was 1840 when Albert first set up a tree in Windsor Castle. In 1848 a picture of the Royal family appeared in the London Illustrated News, they were standing around a decorated fir tree. The Christmas tree had become thoroughly Establishment and was here to stay.

In Britain alone about 8 million pine trees a year are grown for the Christmas market. In total this represents a considerable forest and provides an invaluable, constantly renewed habitat for wildlife such as voles and vole-eaters like long-eared owls and weasels. Most trees grown for Christmas sale are introduced species and don't act as a food plant for many native insects but they do provide undisturbed feeding and nesting areas for larger animals. The majority of agricultural crops are harvested annually, at least with the Christmas tree crop the local wildlife gets to benefit from several years' uninterrupted occupation before the trees are felled.

Plantations of mature alien pine trees support very little wildlife but for the first few years after planting, while sunlight still hits the ground, they are much more benevolent. Christmas tree plantations make perfect habitats for voles. As the trees are not harvested until they are at least four years old, the resident wildlife is left undisturbed for several generations.

For decades the traditional species of Christmas tree bought in Britain was the Norway spruce, although it is a good shape and grows quickly, it has a tendancy to drop its needles as it dries out. Today there are non-drop alternatives and the best-selling tree is now the Nordmann fir, originally found in the Caucasus Mountains of Eastern Europe, which is slightly more expensive but tenaciously retains its needles. The noble fir, from western America, is increasingly popular as it holds onto needles and has a tangy pine scent. The blue spruce, first discovered in the Rocky Mountains, is a soft blue-grey colour and has a punchy, bright citrus scent; although the needles aren't shed they are extremely sharp so this tree shouldn't be used where young children might grab the branches. For small hands a better choice would be the grand fir which has much softer needles and a similar note of citrus.

Small mammals, like voles, attract large predators. Young Christmas tree plantations are excellent hunting grounds for weasels and long-eared owls.

79

Decorated Christmas trees are often sprayed with artificial snow to mimic the winter fir trees found in the Northern Forest.

Poinsettia

Many householders feel that Christmas decorations aren't complete unless there is a healthy poinsettia brightening a shelf or table. Thousands are given every year as gifts but, as the plant originally comes from Mexico, there can't be any direct connection to the nativity itself. The association dates back nearly 500 years when, legends tell, a young Mexican girl wanted to celebrate Jesus' birth by taking a gift to the church, but she was too poor to buy anything of value. An angel spoke to her to say that a gift of weeds collected from the fields would make a perfect gift, if she left them before the alter. The girl

Poinsettia's distinctive red colour doesn't come from its flowers. These are bracts, modified leaves that attract insects to pollinate the real flowers that are small, yellow and rarely noticed.

gathered a posy and carefully took them to church where they miraculously blossomed into the beautiful red bracts of the poinsettia.

In Mexico today the plant is called *Nochebuena*, Spanish for Christmas Eve. The plant didn't get its common name until 1825 when it was claimed by Joel Poinsett, the first American ambassador to Mexico. He introduced the plant to the outside world, along with the story, where it was slowly absorbed into our Christmas flora.

THE ARCTIC CONNECTION
From Turkey to Tundra

Historians teach us that Christmas Day is associated with St Nicholas, the benevolent Bishop of Myra (a town in southern Turkey) who distributed money and gifts to the poor in times of need (although his Saint Day is actually December 6th). He paid the dowries of impoverished girls and gave treats and coins to children — often hiding the gifts in their shoes, left out at night in that very hope. The name Santa Claus itself, first recorded in 1773 via the Dutch term Sinterklaas, comes directly from Saint Nicholas. But if the connection with Nicholas told the whole story surely Santa's elves should be busy making toys in an arid coastal town in the eastern Mediterranean, not in the Arctic tundra? Given this origin, why is Santa customarily depicted in Lapland (northern Scandinavia) or at a secret village somewhere in the region of the North Pole ?

Chronology suggests that St Nicolas himself probably never actually heard of Christmas as a festival. He died in 343 AD and the first known reference to Christmas Day was not until 354 AD. Excepting the name and legendary generosity, St Nicholas has little to do with the modern Santa Claus. The genesis of this mysterious and

magical figure lies much further north in a frozen landscape. The origins of the Santa biography, mysterious and tangled though these are, don't so much come from the forest, rather, they *are* the forest.

Santa's first incarnation was as a living part of the woodland that only emerged in times of great need. He was the spirit of the wood, a kind of Father Nature. He made manifest a promise that the all-powerful forest can provide everything needed in life.

Folklore experts agree that Santa's most important ancestor is thousands of years old and made his home in Scandinavia. Norse mythology contains a shadowy figure known as Allfather, part man, part god, part tree – depending on the story being recounted. Over the centuries Allfather slowly metamorphosed into Odin, the figure folklore expert Margaret Baker calls "the old blue-hooded, cloaked, white-bearded Giftbringer of the north, who rode the midwinter sky on his eight-footed steed Sleipnir, visiting his people with gifts. …" To the touchstones of Allfather, Odin and St Nicolas we can add a glimpse of the shamen of the north lands.

The Scandinavian Arctic in winter challenges the survival of everything living there.

Allfather, in all his guises, was portrayed as an old man with a long white beard. These were the badges of wisdom and longevity.

The indigenous people of the European high north are the Sámi. The Sámi people, also spelled Sami or Saami, inhabit the Arctic area of Sápmi, which encompasses parts of far northern Norway, Sweden, Finland, the Kola Peninsula of Russia, and the border area between south and middle Sweden and Norway. The traditional Sámi are semi-nomadic reindeer herders, tied to the forest and the tundra. The herders lived for much of the time in lavvu, tents similar to the Native American tipi. In bad weather the family would use skins to close the lavvu to keep out the wind and snow. Warmth came from a fire at the centre of the hut and the smoke escaped through a hole in the roof.

At times of ritual or when the weather was at its harshest a shamanic Giftbringer was believed to appear. He would magically enter the hut through the smoke-hole and leave small gifts by the fire.

Allfather had his equivalents in many early cultures. The Saxons had Lord Frost and, even further back, the Green Man. As the cultures met and mixed with the wider world, their beliefs each contributed a little to the modern icon. Slowly over the centuries Allfather, in his many manifestations, and Saint Nicholas melded into one being – Santa Claus from the frozen north.

The Sámi houses in winter camp retain an echo of the lavvu structure.

Depictions of the Allfather character, here called Father Frost, frequently reveal him as a subtle and hidden part of the forest.

One of the key forgotten progenitors of our modern Santa is an American cartoonist by the name of Thomas Nast. In 1869 he created a series of Santa images for the magazine *Harper's Weekly*, which helped to publicize Santa's relocation to the Arctic. Beneath one image was a caption that stated that the old gentleman's home was "near the North Pole, in the ice and snow".

Santa-style

Globally, depictions of Santa – as a portly, jolly, white-bearded man, wearing red coat with white collar and cuffs, white-cuffed red trousers, and black leather belt and shiny black boots – are now largely consistent. In contrast to this red, white and black character, the Allfather figure was believed to be part tree, he wore no clothes and was

The Victorian Santa had a much more varied and colourful wardrobe than he does today.

Thomas Nast's iconic Santa from 1869.

In the trend-setting 1823 poem "Twas The Night Before Christmas" by Clement Clarke Moore, Santa was dressed in furs, while most 19th Century paintings showed him in a long cloak of brown or green, colours that camouflaged him well in the woodland. These outfits are useful clothing for a man of the high forests – but do not match our current image of Santa. The red suit, however, is a very poor choice for someone who wishes to travel discretely around the world unnoticed by sleeping children! Almost anything would be a better camouflage choice than bright red. But Santa's fashion statement has nothing to do with discretion, rather, in part it is the result of the invention of colour printing in the 19th Century. Then as now, Christmas was an important time for retailers and they had to fight to attract customers. Publishers of books, cards and calendars needed to make their goods stand out. On a card a cryptically camouflaged Santa, dressed in brown or green, merging with a forest would attract little attention, so publishers took advantage of a quirky physical function of the human eye.

The primary colours green and red focus at different depths of the retina, when they are used together this tiny distinction produces a small optical illusion, when

protected from the elements by thick bark. For centuries the Father Christmas/Santa figure was depicted as a living part of the forest with twigs and leaves in his hair and beard. These images date back to a time before colour printing, many are woodcuts that make it impossible to work out the hue of Father Christmas' clothes.

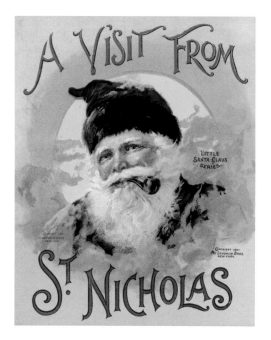

When Father Christmas was first featured on cards, artists couldn't agree what animals pulled his sleigh. On this card it is roe deer, others show horses and goats.

A Visit from St Nicholas was first published, anonymously, in the Troy Sentinel on December 23rd 1823. Publishers soon abandoned Moore's original title and called the poem by its first line Twas the Night Before Christmas.

superimposed they produce a three dimensional effect. The colours seem to be on separate planes. While many earlier images of Santa depict him wearing a variety of colours such as blue, green and yellow, in the new wave of colour printed cards and calendars Santa was shown wearing bright red clothes, simply because they stood out so dramatically against the green backdrop of a forest. The technique is so familiar to us today we barely notice the effect but it was stunning in the Victorian era. The illusion requires that the red object needs to be in front of the green background, so it was guaranteed that holly berries and leaves would also be chosen as subjects for cards. The green/red shift is a highly effective visual trick that gave Father Christmas an entirely new wardrobe.

The Coca-Cola Connection

There is an oft-repeated tale that the modern appearance of Santa was created by Haddon Sundblom, a Swedish artist commissioned to paint an early poster advert for Coca-Cola. But pictures showing Santa in red clothes had been around for several decades before then, although Sundblom certainly helped to clarify and popularise the look. It may seem a minor point but Sundblom's image was the first to show Santa wearing a suit, instead of the traditional long cloak, with a thick black belt. This was a very deliberate detail designed to ensure that Santa's outline exactly mirrored the distinctive wasp-waist of the Coca-Cola bottle. That first poster came out in 1931 and most Santas since have sported a tight black belt.

The final detail of Santa's current incarnation came in 1934 with the song *Santa Claus is Coming to Town*. This ditty contained the lines 'He's making a list and checking it twice", the first ever mention of Santa's dreaded lists of good and bad children. For thousands of years the original gift-giver brought gifts to the needy without passing judgement, while his successor requires fully documented justification. This marks the moment when Santa finally left the great northern forest and stepped into the modern world.

Reindeer

December is the month of the reindeer – images and models of the creatures abound. One survey revealed that reindeer are the best known species of deer in Britain, which is remarkable as in this country there is only one small semi-domesticated herd living in the Cairngorms.

Reindeer come from the Arctic; they live in Norway, Sweden, Finland and Russia. In Old Norse these animals were called 'renn', when the name was absorbed into English we just added the suffix 'deer'. There are an estimated three million reindeer in Scandinavia today and, historically, herding these deer was the key to survival for the Sámi, the indigenous people of the Scandinavian Arctic. A place

Some of the rock carvings at Alta are 6,000 years old and clearly show the importance of reindeer to the inhabitants of the Scandinavian Arctic.

they know as Sápmi but the rest of the world calls Lapland.

Reindeer are grazing animals that thrive in a hostile environment by keeping on the move. They eat leaves and grass but their main food is a lichen known as reindeer moss. The Sámi didn't pen the deer in fields, they guided the deer on seasonal migratory routes as they searched for food. Reindeer walk up to 5,500 kms a year and the Sámi herders simply direct their travels. The deer supplied meat, milk, and clothes in the form of thick pelts that kept out wind, rain and snow, the Sámi even made tools from deer bone and antlers.

There is an equivalent population in Canada and Alaska, but in North America they're called caribou and they're slightly larger than their European counterparts.

Reindeer come in a variety of colours from snow white to a deep chocolate brown. They inhabit the cold Arctic, where snow lies on the ground for half of each year.

Only Sámi children were light enough to ride reindeer over distance.

Reindeer are specialists at surviving in temperatures down to minus 60°C. To help combat the intense cold these deer have two different types of hair, a dense woolly undercoat that acts as a base layer and above this are long, oily guard hairs that keep out wind and snow. Even their breathing is designed to work in Arctic conditions. A blast of ice-cold air easily damages soft lung tissue, so reindeer have a mass of blood vessels in their nose that heat up chilled air before it enters the lungs. When the deer breathes out the same blood vessels absorb heat from the exhaled air, ensuring that the reindeer conserves as much energy as possible

While North American caribou are wild, Scandinavian reindeer are largely semi-domesticated. In 1898 the Canadian Reindeer Project or "Manitoba Expedition" (after the ship on which the Sámi sailed) sought to bring reindeer herding to the Inuit of northern Canada in the hope of building a sustainable industry. On February 28th, 113 reindeer herders - men, women and children from Kautokeino and Karasjok in Norway, 539 draft reindeer, 418 sledges, many dogs and sacks of lichen arrived in New York after crossing the ocean from Bossekop, near Alta on the Norwegian coast. The region of Finnmark surrounding Alta has a long history of herding, carved into rocks at Jiepmaluokta are the world's oldest depictions of reindeer. At nearly 6,000 years of age they reveal scenes of hunting and herding.

The "Manitoba Expedition" herders and reindeer crossed America by train and made their way to Alaska. The convoy attracted much attention throughout their eventful journey with locals lining the route to catch sight of the Sámi and their charges.

The popular 1823 poem "Twas the Night Before Christmas" by Clement Clarke Moore had already stimulated interest in

As they are a semi-domestic species, reindeer are much more approachable than caribou, their cousins in Canada. There are only a few fully wild reindeer in Scandinavia, although there is an introduced population on the other side of the world in South Georgia, close to the Antarctic.

the Sámi and their reindeer, launching many of the modern conceptions of the Santa and reindeer story. By the 1920s there were 100,000 reindeer in Alaska and one U.S. businessman, Carl Lomen, set out to market the reindeer and their connection to Santa to the American public:

"To promote the sale of reindeer meat and furs, Lomen and Company collaborate with Macy's Department Stores to stage annual Christmas parades with Santa Clauses and teams of reindeer driven by Sámi and Native herders from Alaska. Matthis Ivar Klementsen Nillika is the

For moving light loads Sámi herders used pulks, small sledges pulled by just one reindeer. Larger sledges had teams of up to 12 deer.

first Santa. These parades extend into the 1930s. Participating cities include Portland, St. Paul, Boston, San Francisco, Chicago, Seattle and Brooklyn. The Lomen brothers write fake children's letters asking about Santa Claus, which are published in U.S. newspapers. Because of the letters and the parades, Santa Claus and reindeer become an integral part of the North American Christmas story". (From *Baiki, the North American Sámi Journal*)

Reindeer are unique in that both males and females have antlers, in every other deer species only the males have them as signals of power, health and dominance. As male deer are bigger and stronger than females, when food is short they easily drive off the females to feed. But in the harsh Arctic environment this imbalance would often be fatal so, in reindeer, evolution has intervened to even the match. To compensate for their lack of bulk, females maintain their antlers during the worst weather, while the males drop theirs much earlier. The males have size and strength on their side, while the smaller females are equipped with weapons.

This leads us to a conundrum, traditionally Santa's sleigh is pulled by eight healthy male deer. Each animal, harnessed to the sleigh with its mountain of presents, boasts a fine set of antlers. But, by the end of December, all the male reindeer should have lost theirs so, inescapably, every single deer in the team must be female!

There is a post script to this biological detail. The Sámi often castrate male

A male reindeer at Christmas. The new antlers will start to grow again in spring from buds, called pedicles, on the top of his head. Reindeer antlers are bony growths that sprout and fall every year. They are very different to horns which are permanent and grow in tandem with the animal.

reindeer that are used to pull sleighs, as it makes them more docile. This has the side-effect of ensuring the males do not drop their antlers at the normal time, rather, they fall much later. It is just possible that the Christmas Eve reindeer are castrated males, adding authenticity to the Sámi origin of this facet of Santa's adventures.

Flying Reindeer ?

In North America, sledges are pulled by husky dogs and Malamutes, Scandinavia is the only place where reindeer are traditionally harnessed to the sleigh or *pulk*. A pulk is a low-slung, small toboggan used for transport, pulled by a dog or a skier, or in Lapland pulled by reindeer. There is strong evidence that reindeer were the first grazing animals to be domesticated, long before cattle or sheep. Reindeer stand waist-high to an adult herder and have backbones that are not strong enough to be ridden over distance, but their short legs are powerful

Fly agaric's unmistakeable colour is a warning sign that the fungus contains potentially dangerous chemicals. It was once thought that the fungus earned its name because it was used in a homemade potion that killed flies. But many etymologists now believe that the word 'fly' comes from the medieval belief that hallucinations are caused when flies enter the human head and cause the senses to misbehave.

and designed to walk for many hours a day through the deepest snow. Perfect physical qualities for pulling a load fitted with sledge runners.

Nowadays the Sámi use snowmobiles, 4x4 vehicles and helicopters to move around their deer grazing lands but their ancestors pulled everything they owned on sleighs.

Life is harsh and difficult in a northern winter, the sun can entirely disappear for three months and the temperature plummets. During this time the reindeer and Sámi herders leave the coast, the mountains and open tundra and withdraw inland to the lowlands and forest where conditions are less challenging and there is usually more to eat. This is when the weakest deer are culled, to provide meat for the herders and ensure that the scarce supplies of moss go to the strongest deer, giving them the best chance of survival.

Historically, once the berries and nuts of autumn had been exhausted, reindeer meat was the only available food for the Sámi. In many other cultures these long cold winter days often resulted in an increase in alcohol consumption but not in the Arctic because there it's just too cold to ferment a brew. Indigenous people of the high north had no access to intoxicating drinks until they were brought in from further south. However, long ago, the reindeer herders discovered another way of easing the grim realities of winter – the mushroom!

In late autumn reindeer eat a variety of food, to build up their body weight ready for the onset of bad weather. Some of their favourites are the mushrooms that grow in the vast forests. A few are poisonous and are left strictly alone, others are harmless and are eaten with enthusiasm. And one is very strange indeed. The most distinctive fungus in the forest goes by the scientific name of *Amanita muscaria* – the fly agaric. It is the toadstool of fairytale books, with a scarlet cap that is peppered with splashes of white.

There is a myth that toadstools are poisonous and mushrooms are edible, but this is untrue. Botanically there is no distinction between mushroom and toadstool, they are both fungi. Eaten in quantity fly agaric can be fatal but in small amounts it has an effect that is not unwelcome.

The Sámi noticed that after eating the garish mushrooms reindeer would start to behave oddly. They became uncoordinated, stumbled and even toppled over, however the deer appeared to instinctively know when to stop consuming and afterwards would quickly recover. It seems that some reindeer enjoy fly agaric so much that they will fight for a chance to eat these mushrooms. Experienced herders used to carry fly agaric in their hands to get unruly deer to follow them.

At some unknown point in history the herders themselves begun eating the fungus but alongside recreational use, they used its intoxicating properties in a special way – this was one of the tools used by Sámi shamen to enable them to commune with their spirit guides. As there are no written Sámi records or documents that date back earlier than the 18th Century, it's not possible to calculate exactly when this originated. The details may have been lost but we do know that the Sámi people learned how to minimise the potentially dangerous effects of fly agaric in

Eating just a little fly agaric could make reindeer appear very strange to the eye.

surprising ways.

The active agent in fly agaric is a compound called *muscimol*, a psychoactive drug that causes hallucinations. Drying the fungus before eating it reduces the levels of toxins present in the drug and increases its hallucinogenic effect on the brain. The Sámi also have a custom of feeding fly agaric to their deer and collecting the intoxicated deer's urine to drink. The reindeer's digestive system metabolises the more toxic components of the toadstool, leaving urine with the hallucinogenic elements of the fungus intact. Drinking the urine gives a 'high' similar to taking LSD.

Many travellers over the centuries have lived with the Sámi and recorded their experiences of trying the fungus. The reports all have one thing in common. Within a very short time everything nearby appears to take on a life of its own, and often starts to move unexpectedly.

American Jonathan Otts is an expert in the use and abuse of plants and, having eaten fungus loaded with muscimols wrote " I noticed that I was experiencing changes in visual perception. These effects became stronger over the next hour, and were characterized by sensing an 'alive quality' in inanimate objects, a wavy motion in the visual field like the brushwork on a Van Gogh canvas".

Under the visionary effects of the drink, the Sámi believed their reindeer were flying through space, and looking down on the world from a shifted perspective. According to some observers, the reindeer's fondness for toadstool highs is such that they, in turn, have been known to eat the snow on which intoxicated humans have urinated.

Fly agaric grows widely in the Scandinavian forest but not in any great quantity. The dried fungus had to be taken sparingly if it was to last throughout the long winter. We know that the Sámi customarily used it only during rituals and when times were harsh, when lack of food and weather conspired to make life very difficult. In the winter camps, where Sámi were surrounded by reindeer, it is not difficult to imagine how the herds might look under an Aurora sky - flying in a swirl of hooves to a chorus of neck-bells worn by the lead deer. Could this be the origin of Santa's flying reindeer?

In Siberia Sámi shamen wore special robes to collect the fly agaric mushrooms. Their coats and trousers were red with the collar and cuffs trimmed with white fur, to mimic the colour scheme of their revered fungi. The shaman collected the fly agaric in a special sack, then returned to camp and entered the lavvu through the smoke hole on the roof.

This was followed by a ritual during which the shaman ate and shared the sacred mushrooms with the participants. The smoke hole became a portal into the spiritual world where the people focused their visions.

So we have a wise shaman dressed in red descending a chimney from the wintery night and bringing the gift of visions to a waiting family. Meanwhile, outside the lavvu, reindeer move magically above the snow.

THE PERFECT CHRISTMAS EVE
- Santa's Team is born

The names of Santa's reindeer are Dancer, Prancer, Dasher and Vixen. Comet, Cupid, Dunder (that's right, the spelling was later changed to Donder and finally we settled for Donner) and Blixem – which slowly evolved into Blitzen.

The names come from a poem written in 1823 by Clement Clarke Moore, a professor of Oriental and Greek Literature in New York. Its original title was "A Visit from St Nicholas" but most people today know it simply as "Twas The Night Before Christmas".

Legend tells that Moore wrote the poem following a long winter sleigh ride that was almost certainly powered by horses. Moore was an American but he chose European reindeer to pull the poem's sleigh rather than the caribou that were native to his home continent. Moore's poem crystallized a vision of Santa Claus, reindeer and Christmas Eve that persists to this day.

A Visit from St. Nicholas

'Twas the night before Christmas,
when all thro' the house
Not a creature was stirring, not even a mouse;
The stockings were hung by the chimney with care,
In hopes that St. Nicholas soon would be there;
The children were nestled all snug in their beds,
While visions of sugar plums
danc'd in their heads,
And Mama in her 'kerchief, and I in my cap,
Had just settled our brains
for a long winter's nap -
When out on the lawn there arose such a clatter,
I sprang from the bed to see what was the matter.
Away to the window I flew like a flash,
Tore open the shutters, and threw up the sash.
The moon on the breast of the new fallen snow,
Gave the luster of mid-day to objects below;
When, what to my wondering eyes should appear,
But a miniature sleigh, and eight tiny reindeer,
With a little old driver, so lively and quick,
I knew in a moment it must be St. Nick.
More rapid than eagles his coursers they came,
And he whistled, and shouted,
and call'd them by name:

"Now! Dasher, now!
Dancer, now! Prancer and Vixen,
On! Comet, on! Cupid, on! Donder and Blitzen;
To the top of the porch! To the top of the wall!
Now dash away! Dash away! Dash away all!"
As dry leaves that before the wild hurricane fly,
When they meet with an obstacle,
mount to the sky;
So up to the house-top the coursers they flew,
With the sleigh full of toys - and St. Nicholas too:
And then in a twinkling, I heard on the roof
The prancing and pawing of each little hoof.
As I drew in my head, and was turning around,
Down the chimney St. Nicholas
came with a bound:
He was dress'd all in fur, from his head to his foot,
And his clothes were all tarnish'd
with ashes and soot;
A bundle of toys was flung on his back,
And he look'd like a peddler just opening his pack:
His eyes - how they twinkled!
His dimples: how merry,
His cheeks were like roses,
his nose like a cherry;

His droll little mouth was drawn up like a bow,
And the beard of his chin was as white as the snow;
The stump of a pipe he held tight in his teeth,
And the smoke it encircled his head like a wreath.
He had a broad face,
and a little round belly
That shook when he laugh'd,
like a bowl full of jelly:
He was chubby and plump,
a right jolly old elf,
And I laugh'd when I saw him in spite of myself;
A wink of his eye and a twist of his head
Soon gave me to know I had nothing to dread.
He spoke not a word, but went straight to his work,
And fill'd all the stockings; then turn'd with a jerk,
And laying his finger aside of his nose
And giving a nod, up the chimney he rose.
He sprung to his sleigh,
to his team gave a whistle,
And away they all flew,
like the down of a thistle:
But I heard him exclaim,
ere he drove out of sight -
Happy Christmas to all,
and to all a good night.

Clement Clarke Moore

Rudolph

Sadly Rudolph is not one of Santa's original reindeer. He was invented by a minor advertising copywriter called Robert L May in 1939, an employee of the department store Montgomery Ward & Co in Chicago.

Every year the store bought and gave away colouring books as small Christmas gifts to its customers, but that year management decided to create and publish their own gift books in order to publicise the store. May was given the job of producing the book and decided on a deer as the main character, mainly because his four-year old daughter, Barbara, was particularly entranced by the deer at Chicago Zoo. For the first book, May wrote a poem, in rhyming couplets, about the adventures of a lonely misfit deer with a very unusual nose, he gave it the title "Rudolph, the red-nosed reindeer" and a copy was given to every child who visited Santa in the store.

Customers loved it and more than 2 million copies were distributed. The story was soon nationally famous and was adapted and set to music in 1948 by May's brother-in-law, songwriter Johnny Marks. 'Rudolph' has since gone on to become the second highest selling Christmas song in history, eclipsed only by 'White Christmas'.

His is also the name that most immediately crops up when people try to remember Santa's team, even though he was never an official member.

Incidentally, May originally called his reindeer Reginald, but his daughter preferred Rudolph, so the name was changed at the last moment.

Twelve Days of Christmas

On the twelfth day of Christmas,
my true love sent to me
Twelve drummers drumming,
Eleven pipers piping,
Ten lords a-leaping,
Nine ladies dancing,
Eight maids a-milking,
Seven swans a-swimming,
Six geese a-laying,
Five golden rings,
Four calling birds,
Three French hens,
Two turtle doves,
And a partridge in a pear tree!

The word blackbird is relatively new. In Old English these birds were called ouzels. Later they were known as collie-birds, possibly from the description coal-black. Female blackbirds are chocolate coloured and even the males aren't truly black, but very dark brown.

This is one of the most familiar of all Christmas songs and first appeared in Britain, without music, as a catchy chant in a 1780 children's book called *Mirth Without Mischief*. Its origins are French and it is probably much older than the 18th Century.

Some people read cryptic messages into the lyrics but most historians believe that it is simply a memory song, like 'One Man Went to Mow', used to pass the time during Christmas celebrations. Each singer had to contribute a line, in the right order, and the first to forget had to pay a small forfeit. The words are thought to refer to the preparations involved for the huge parties that were once held on January 6th - also known as Twelfth Night. The drummers, pipers, Lords and Ladies describe the dancers and musicians that provided the entertainment. Eight-maids-

Pheasants are not a species native to Britain, they were first introduced by the Romans and then later the Normans. They were rare until the 18th Century when gamekeepers wiped out huge numbers of predators to ensure good hauls for the newly created shooting estates. This allowed pheasants to multiply rapidly and become an integral part of the countryside.

Turtle doves were once a familiar bird of the British countryside, but in recent years they have become very rare.

a-milking acknowledged the importance of dairy delicacies on any feast day - cheese, buttermilk and custard played a big part in all celebrations. Milk was plentiful and versatile, it was essential at Christmas. Some of the other references are a little less obvious.

Five gold rings. This is an old name for the common pheasant. Although it is now an established part of the countryside these birds are not native to Britain, they were introduced from India via southern Europe and were quite rare until the 18th Century. As they were interlopers we obviously had no English word for the new arrivals, in many places they were named after one distinguishing feature - the thin ring of light feathers around their neck. For nearly 200 years these birds were known as 'gold rings' or sometimes just 'golds'. Five gold rings simply means five pheasants.

Four colly birds. Although many people

sing 'calling birds', in the original published version the gift was 'four colly birds' – the traditional name for blackbirds. In Britain 'colly' was an old term for black, coming from the word coal. When the song became popular in America the word 'colly' wasn't understood, the Americans changed it to 'calling' and shipped their version back to us.

For many centuries people exchanged gifts on each of the 12 days of Christmas, not just confining the ritual to one day as we do now. Small items of food were the most usual offering. This song is a party plan complete with menu and suggested entertainment. French hens are a kind of chicken, while blackbirds, doves and swans are all prized edible birds that for centuries featured in lavish Christmas feasts, special treats that would only be served on important occasions.

Partridges, served in a sweetened pear sauce, were particularly popular.

Despite the song, partridges spend almost all of their lives on the ground. There are two resident species in Britain. This is the native grey partridge, the red-legged partridge was introduced from mainland Europe in the 17th Century. The newcomer is now a more common species than our original resident.

"I am the Ghost of Christmas Present. Look upon me! You have never seen the like of me before!"

Charles Dickens' masterpiece *A Christmas Carol* was published on 19ᵗʰ December 1843. Cultural experts believe that this short book, more than anything else in history, influenced the way we celebrate Christmas in Britain today. At that time Christmas trees and turkeys were only just becoming popular and, coincidentally, the book came out in the same year as the first commercial Christmas card. Until that time carol singing was unknown outside churches, it was the early Victorians that took festive songs out into the street and into houses. With typically observant intelligence, Dickens skilfully wove these radical new features into his book. He wrote *A Christmas Carol* in just six weeks, it may have only contained five chapters but was a colossal international success that has never once been out of print.

Victorian celebrations weren't always the quiet, sober events we believe them to be.

Charles Dickens. "And it was always said of him, that he knew how to keep Christmas well, if any man alive possessed the knowledge. May that be truly said of us, and all of us!"
A Christmas Carol.

Even more importantly it was enormously popular with ordinary people. Dickens was working at a time when new systems of mass communication were being developed. Suddenly books weren't the sole privilege of the wealthy, modern publishing methods had reduced the cover price and books became accessible to many, for just a few pennies.

Until the middle of the 19th Century each part of the country had its own unique Christmas traditions, unaffected by the strange habits of folk living 550 kms away. Christmas in Cornwall was a very different festival to Christmas in Northumberland. Books and magazines changed the way we saw the world, new ideas and fashions were carried to even the most remote village. The widespread success of Dickens' story encouraged readers to copy the latest London trends, and for the first time every ingredient for a thoroughly modern Christmas was listed together in one best-selling book. Carols, turkeys, gifts, snow, a full day off from work, family gatherings, decorated trees, charitable donations, good food and drink, dancing and games – the catalogue goes on. Charles Dickens brought together the elements and defined Christmas as we know it. Cultural commentators agree that it really is impossible to overstate the importance of *A Christmas Carol* in the way we celebrate the festival in the 21st Century.

Thomas Hood, the Victorian poet and humorist wrote "If Christmas, with its ancient and hospitable customs, its social and charitable observances, were ever in danger of decay, this is the book that would give them a new lease."

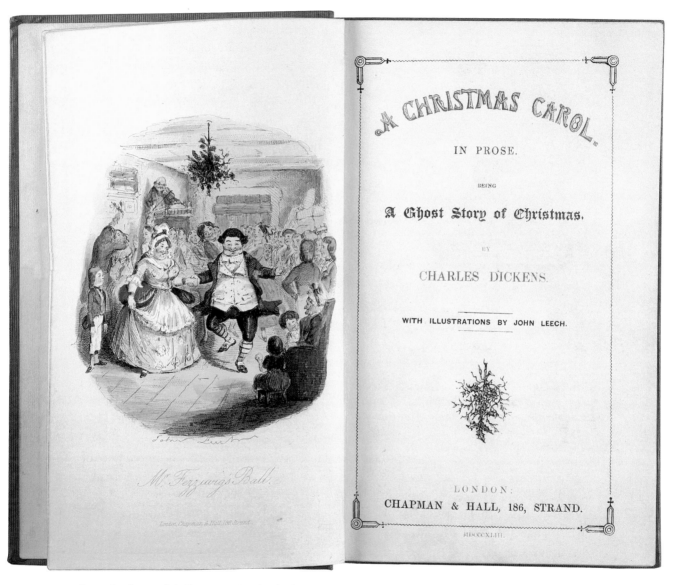

An early edition of A Christmas Carol. The first print run of 6,000 books sold out in less than a week. It has since been turned into plays, films, and musicals. The words Scrooge and humbug have become part of our modern language.

Which Brings us to Snow...

A crisp, snowy rural landscape is one of the most familiar images on cards and calendars, but a white Christmas is a truly rare event in Britain. For most of the country snow, if any falls at all, tends to arrive in the early part of the New Year rather than mid-December. People may dream about a white Christmas but few actually experience them. Like so many other invented minutiae of the season, we really need to look at Dickens' influence to determine its provenance.

Charles John Huffam Dickens was born in Portsmouth on 7th February 1812. The year is important because Britain, along with most of Europe, was then coming to the end of a mini Ice Age. This was a period of cooling when the world's average temperature dropped, creating longer and harsher winters. It lasted 300 years and resulted in a succession of ruined crops, frozen lakes, high animal and human death rates and unusually deep snow falls that stayed on the ground for many weeks. Temperatures remained below zero for months. It was so cold that the Thames often completely froze; Londoners took full advantage of these occasions and held impromptu fairs on river ice that could be half a metre deep. In his entry for 1683 diarist John Evelyn describes London's first Frost Fair:

"Coaches plied from Westminster to the Temple, and from several other stairs too and fro, as in the streets; sleds, sliding with skeetes, a bull-baiting, horse and coach races, puppet plays and interludes, cooks, tipling and other lewd places, so that it seemed to be a bacchanalian triumph, or carnival on the water".

There was bull-baiting on the ice, skating and puppet shows. Traders set up stalls selling hot chestnuts, roast beef and wine. But they had to keep a close eye on the temperature; sudden thaws were responsible for much lost merchandise and many deaths.

Frost Fairs were unofficial events and the

last spontaneously started on 1ˢᵗ February 1814 and continued for just four days. The ice was so strong that it supported an elephant walking over the Thames near Blackfriars Bridge. Because climate change is a slow process it's impossible to give a precise date for the end of the Mini Ice-Age but meteorologists usually say that it finished around 1850. This means that the first half of the 19ᵗʰ Century experienced long hard winters with plenty of snow. That's the period during which Charles Dickens, the architect of the modern festivities, was growing up and working. In his two most influential seasonal books, *Pickwick Papers* and *A Christmas Carol*, Dickens wrote about snow on Christmas Day because that was exactly what he'd experienced.

In the 20ᵗʰ Century there were just two years, 1938 and 1981, when the majority of people in Britain enjoyed a white Christmas Day. In the first 24 years of Dickens' life, he probably lived through nine. As he so often did, Dickens used these personal experiences in his books. As the most influential living author of the day, many of his references were quickly picked up by other media and soon became part of the Christmas tradition - in images at least. Of course it helps that snow is picturesque,

dramatic and also builds atmosphere. Those early images had a power and impetus of their own. In the same way that in the children's poem 'Humpty Dumpty' there is no mention of eggs, but whenever the rhyme is illustrated, Humpty is always portrayed as an egg - there's no immediate logic to this association, but isn't that part of the legacy of faded past traditions? We maintain our shifting rituals because generations before us found them meaningful, shaped them, carried them out and handed them on to us. Just like the picture of a cosy white Christmas.

It's useful to remember that in Bethlehem, where the original nativity is set, the average temperature in December is around 10°C, which is far too warm for snow. The majority of people who celebrate Christmas around the world never experience snow in their home country. Bing Crosby's legendary song *White Christmas* was written in 1940 by Irving Berlin, sitting in southern California where snow usually doesn't fall for decades. The song sold millions of copies and snowy scenes still appear on cards and calendars around the world, sent to and from people who have never seen a snow-blanketed morning. And for this, in part, we thank Mr. Dickens.

The natural history of Christmastide in the 21st Century is a complicated palimpsest. It draws on customs, food, beliefs and images from almost every area of the world. They have been gathered and adapted over possibly 3500 years and the resulting festivities connect distant cultures in ways that nothing else does. Now surely that is something truly worth celebrating.

"Happy Christmas to all, and to all a good-night".
Clement Clarke Moore
Twas the Night Before Christmas

To Delve More Deeply…

Abbot, Elizabeth (2010). *Sugar – A Bittersweet History.* Gerald Duckworth.

Armstrong, Edward A. (1970). *The Folklore of Birds.* Dover Publications.

Baker, Margaret (2007). *Discovering Christmas Customs and Folklore: A Guide to Seasonal Rites Throughout the World.* Shire.

Baker, Margaret (2008). *Discovering the Folklore of Plants.* Shire.

Black, Maggie (2012). *The Medieval Cookbook.* British Museum Press.

Broomfield, Andrea (2007). *Food and Cooking in Victorian England: A History.* Greenwood Publishing.

Coe, Sophie and Michael (2013). *The True History of Chocolate.* Thames and Hudson.

Curtis, Wayne (2007). *And a Bottle of Rum: A History of the New World in Ten Cocktails.* Three Rivers Press.

Dickens, Charles (1995). *Christmas Books.* Wordsworth.

Elmes James (1826). *A General and Bibliographical Dictionary of the Fine Arts, London.* Thomas Tegg.

Evans, Robert C. (1994). *Jonson and the Contexts of His Time.* Bucknell University Press.

Forbes, R. J. (1970). *A Short History of the Art of Distillation from the Beginnings up to the Death of Cellier Blumenthal.* BRILL.

Grocock, Christoper and Granger, Sally (2006). *Apicius: A Critical Edition with an Introduction and English Translation.* Prospect Books.

Harding, Patrick (2007). *The Christmas Book: A Treasury of Festive Facts.* John Blake Publishing.

Highfield, Roger (2002). *Can Reindeer Fly? The Science of Christmas.* Phoenix.

Hillier, Bevis (1982). *Greetings From Christmas Past.* Herbert Press.

Hutton, Ronald (1996). *The Stations of the Sun: A History of the Ritual Year in Britain.* Oxford University Press.

Kelly, Richard - ed (2003). *A Christmas Carol by Charles Dickens*. Broadview Editions.

Kent, Neil (2013.) *The Sámi Peoples of the North: A Social and Cultural History*. C. Hurst & Co.

Moore, Clement C. (2004). *The Night Before Christmas*. Harper Collins.

Morris, Desmond (1992). *Christmas Watching*. Jonathan Cape.

O'Donoghue, Heather (2008). *From Asgard to Valhalla: The Remarkable History of the Norse Myths*. Tauris.

Panathi, Charles (1989). *Extraordinary Origins of Everyday Things*. HarperPerennial.

Paterson, Jacqueline Memory (2011). *Tree Wisdom: The definitive guidebook to the myth, folklore and healing power of Trees*. Thorsons.

Renfrew, Jane (1985). *Food and Cooking in Roman Britain: History and Recipes*. English Heritage.

Smith Delia (2004). *Delia's Winter Collection*. BBC Books; New Ed edition.

Smith, Tilly. (2006). *The Real Rudolph: A Natural History of the Reindeer*. Sutton Publishing.

Struthers, Jane (2012). *The Book of Christmas*. Ebury Press.

Tomalin, Claire (2012). *Charles Dickens: A Life*. Penguin.

Toussaint-Samat, Maguelonne (2008). *History of Food*. Wiley Blackwell.

Turner, Jack (2011). *Spice: The History of a Temptation*. Harper Perennial.

Wilson, C. Anne (2003). *Food and Drink in Britain: From the Stone Age to the 19th Century*. Academy Chicago Publishers.

Websites
www.baiki.org
Báiki is a major English-language source of information about Sámi arts, literature, history, spirituality, and environmental concerns.

INDEX